D1623732

Marcel Duchamp

Thames and Hudson

709.44

HAVERING COLLEGE
OF FURTHER HIGHER EDUCATION
LEARNING RESOURCES
CENTRE

112113

This book has been published
on the occasion of the exhibition
Marcel Duchamp
Palazzo Grassi, San Samuele 3231, Venice
April-July 1993

First published in Great Britain in 1993
by Thames and Hudson Ltd, London

© 1993 Gruppo Editoriale Fabbri
Bompiani, Sonzogno, Etas S.p.A, Milan

All Rights Reserved. No part of this publication may
be reproduced or transmitted in any form or by any
means, electronic or mechanical, including photocopy,
recording or any other information storage and retrieval
system, without prior permission in writing from the
publisher

Printed and bound in Milan, Italy, by Gruppo Editoriale
Fabbri, Bompiani, Sonzogno, Etas S.p.A.

Marcel Duchamp is undeniably one of twentieth-century art's most important and enigmatic figures. His art works and his writings make him a leading cultural figure not just of our own but of all time, while his revolutionary, creative propositions force us to think in a new way and to reach beyond the traditional border lines that define Art and the role of Art in society. Duchamp indeed was the first to prove that an artist need not limit himself to any single means of expression.

Duchamp's experiments with central perspective, with the "fourth dimension" and with movement led us into formerly unknown territory, changed the way we think about images and form. Eventually, they were to become a significant element in the artistic renewal of the Forties and Fifties.

In some of his books, Duchamp traced a fundamental map of the intimate relations and the extraordinary coherence of his artistic opus.

This exhibition and its catalogue attempt to take into account the hints and pointers that emerge from Duchamp's own writings and so give us a better insight into his works.

This project could not have reached completion without the support of Alexina Duchamp. In addition to her personal contribution as a connoisseur of her husband's works, Madame Duchamp also helped Palazzo Grassi obtain the loan of important works, some of which might not have been available without her assistance.

I should like to offer my warmest thanks to Madame Duchamp and to all those who have worked to create this great exhibition.

Giovanni Agnelli

PALAZZOGRASSI

Comitato Amici
di Palazzo Grassi

President
Feliciano Benvenuti

Vice President
Giuseppe Donegà

Director of Cultural Programmes
Paolo Viti

Director of the Administration
Pasquale Bonagura

President
Susanna Agnelli

Committee
Marella Agnelli
Umberto Agnelli
Mirella Barracco
Vittore Branca
Cristiana Brandolini D'Adda
Francesco Cingano
Attilio Codognato
Giancarlo Ferro
Gianluigi Gabetti
Knud W. Jensen
Michel Laclotte
Giancarlo Ligabue
Pietro Marzotto
Thomas Messer
Philippe de Montebello
Sabatino Moscati
Giovanni Nuvoletti Perdomini
Richard E. Oldenburg
Giuseppe Panza di Biumo
Alfonso Emilio Pérez Sánchez
Claude Pompidou
Maurice Rheims
Cesare Romiti
Norman Rosenthal
Guido Rossi
Francesco Valcanover
Mario Valeri Manera
Bruno Visentini
Bruno Zevi

Secretary of the Committee
Furio Colombo

Palazzo Grassi S.p.A.
San Samuele 3231, Venice

This exhibition devoted to Marcel Duchamp represents a link in the ongoing cultural itinerary which Palazzo Grassi has been following from the outset, offering a variety of themes spanning from archaeology, the Renaissance and Modern Art, to the contemporary masters.

The scope of each exhibition has been to shed light on themes which have not received the attention they deserve, or which provide new insights into the so-called anti-classical cultures, such as that of the Celts, or the Futurists, whom Duchamp dubbed "non-artists".

Duchamp was in fact the first artist to stray off-limits, to venture off the paper's edge and outside the picture space, breaking out of the hackneyed frames of reference and raising commonplace objects to the ranks of "works of art". For this reason he is considered the Father of the avant-garde, for having successfully shifted our attention from the business of artistic creation to the concept underlying art itself. The critical rediscovery of Duchamp took place in the Fifties and Sixties, when he suddenly became a point of reference for all the new movements as they emerged: Pop Art, Conceptual Art, and Minimalism.

In the case of the present exhibition, Palazzo Grassi has set itself the task of presenting Duchamp's work as exhaustively as possible, following its development through each of the main movements of this century – Cubism, Fauvism, Dadaism and Surrealism – with the hope that these efforts will contribute to a better understanding of that contemporary art which is, inevitably, and expression of our own culture, the culture of our daily existence. But it is also the expression of our striving forwards, towards a future which is ultimately tied to the present and the past – in a word: an exhibition which aims to draw our attention to the very way of being of our civilization.

Feliciano Benvenuti

Acknowledgements

A great number of individuals and institutions have made this exhibition possible.
I would like first of all to thank Alexina Duchamp, who has helped in many different ways
and at all stages in the development of the project for the exhibition and its catalogue.
Jackie Monnier who, since the Sixties helped Marcel Duchamp by assembling new boxes of the
portable museum, *La Boîte-en-Valise*, and who knows the work in great detail, has also
provided information and assistance at all levels.
Jacques Caumont and Jennifer Gough-Cooper whose studies of the work and life of Marcel
Duchamp have brought light to the exhibition in Palazzo Grassi and its catalogue. A clarity
reigns which in no way imposes an interpretation.
Ulf Linde has once more put his passionate interest and knowledge to work and produced the
splendid revised version of the Large Glass for the exhibition.
Richard Hamilton has again proved his affection for the work of Marcel Duchamp and helped
embellish the exhibition. He has permitted us to use extracts from his typographic version of
the notes from the Green Box in English, which we can also see transposed into Italian.
André Raffray has provided his artistic talent once more for the presentation of the
readymades.
Many museums have agreed to lend important works and I would like to thank most heartily
all the directors and curators who have helped the exhibition by lending their treasures.
My special thanks go to Anne d'Harnoncourt of the Philadelphia Museum of Art, who has the
largest collection of the works of Marcel Duchamp. Without her interest and blessing no
serious exhibition of Marcel Duchamp can be achieved.
Bjorn Springfeldt of the Moderna Museet in Stockholm showed once more the great generosity
which has made other sections of the exhibition possible, especially those concerned with the
Large Glass and *Etant donnés....*
Other very important loans have come from:
Mary Gardner Neill, Yale University Art Gallery, Yale; Richard Oldenburg and Kirk Varnedoe,
The Museum of Modern Art, New York; Thomas Krens, The Solomon R. Guggenheim Museum,
New York; Philip Rylends of the Peggy Guggenheim Collection, Venice; Eliane de Wilde,
Musées Royaux des Beaux-Arts, Brussells; Annie Angremy, Bibliothèque Nationale, Paris;
François Chapon, Bibliothèque Littéraire Jacques Doucet, and all the other libraries, very
numerous, that have generously provided material for the biography.
Amongst private individuals who have helped, many prefer to remain anonymous. My most sincere
thanks go to all of them and particularly to Angelo Calmarini, Milan; Attilio Codognato,
Venice; Jean-Jacques Lebel, Paris; Arturo Schwarz, Milan; Robert Shapazian, Los Angeles.

Pontus Hulten

Acknowledgment is made to the following for permission to quote:

Amherst, Amherst College Library

Austin, Harry Ransom Humanities Research Center, The University of Texas at Austin

Azay-le-Rideau, Mme Aube Elléouët

Berkeley, The Bancroft Library, University of California at Berkeley

Blainville-Crevon, Xavier Le Bertre

Bologna, Dino Gavina

Boston, Institute of Contemporary Art

Cambridge, The Schlesinger Library, Radcliffe College

Carbondale, Morris Library, Southern Illinois University at Carbondale

Chicago, The Art Institute of Chicago Archives

Chicago, The Newberry Library

Claremont, The Arensberg Archives at the Francis Bacon Library

Fribourg, Claude Blancpain

Haimhausen
Ursula and Klaus-Peter Bergmann

Hempstead, Hofstra University

Houston, Museum of Fine Arts

Houston, William Camfield

Les Laumes, Mme Marie Gorsline

London, Anthony Hill

London, Arts Council of Great Britain

London, Richard Hamilton

Milan, Arturo Schwarz

Milan, Enrico Baj

Munich, Dr. Wieland Schmied

New Haven, The Beinecke Rare Book and Manuscript Library, Yale University

New Haven, Ursula Lawder

New York, Alfred Knopf

New York, Arne H. Ekstrom

New York, George Staempfli

New York, Monique Fong

New York, Mrs Lillian Kiesler

New York, Mrs Noma Copley

New York, Museum of Modern Art Archives

New York, New York Public Library

New York, Rare Book and Manuscript Library, Columbia University

New York, The American Academy and Institute of Art and Letters

New York, The Solomon R. Guggenheim Museum

New York, Timothy Baum

Ojai, Beatrice Wood

Paris, Alain Mounier

Paris, Bernard Dumouchel

Paris, Bibliothèque Littéraire Jacques Doucet

Paris, Daniel Spoerri

Paris, Documentation du Musée National d'Art Moderne, Centre Georges Pompidou

Paris, Fondation Jean Dubuffet

Paris, Galerie Louis Carré

Paris, Jean-Jacques Lebel

Paris, Jean Suquet

Paris, Mme Elisa Breton

Paris, Mme Jacques Savy

Paris, Mme Natalia Istrati

Pasadena, Norton Simon Museum

Philadelphia, Philadelphia Museum of Art

Pittsburgh, The Carnegie Museum of Art

Portland, Portland Museum of Art

Rome, Gianfranco Baruchello

Rouen, Mme Françoise Menuisement

Rouen, Musée des Beaux-Arts

San Francisco, San Francisco Museum of Modern Art

Santa Monica, The Getty Center for the History of Art and the Humanities

Sintra, Mimi Fogt

Stuttgart, Staatsgalerie

The Hague, Gemeentemuseum

Tulsa, McFarlin Library, The University of Tulsa

Washington, Archives of American Art, Smithsonian Institution

Washington, The Philips Collection Archives

Williamstown, George Heard Hamilton

Zurich, Doris Stauffer

Zurich, Hans Bolliger

also to Simon Watson Taylor for his English translation of "Phare de la Mariée" by André Breton, and to Barbara Wright for her translation into English of the texts from *Littérature* by André Breton and many other friends of Marcel Duchamp and colleagues who have provided information and material for these Ephemerides.

Exhibition Committee   Catalogue

Chief Curator
Pontus Hulten

Exhibition Curator
Jacques Caumont
Assistant
Pierre Astier

with the collaboration of
Ida Gianelli
Director, Castello di Rivoli
Museo di Arte Contemporanea

Palazzo Grassi Secretariat
Clarenza Catullo
Francesca Pattaro
Marina Scozzi
Paola Trevisan

Paris Secretariat
Nathalie Meneau

Press Relations
Andrea Ranghieri

Project
Gae Aulenti
with Francesca Fenaroli

Graphic Design
Pierluigi Cerri
with Olivier Maupas
and Beatrice Lancini

Lighting Design
Piero Castiglioni

Shadows for the Readymades
André Raffray

Editorial Director
Mario Andreose

Graphic Design
Pierluigi Cerri
with Andrea Lancellotti
and Luca Dotti
Costanza Melli
Sara Ricciardi

Coordinating Editor
Simonetta Rasponi

Editorial staff
Paula Billingsley
Claudia Converso
Enrica Sacchi
Gilberta Stivanin

Iconographic Research
Carla Viazzoli
with Evelina Rossetti

Production staff
Edo Albini
Carla Bonacina
Silvano Caldara
Giuseppina Magro
Roberto Moroni
Carla Regonesi
Enrico Vida

Secretary
Luisa Gandolfi

Editing and pagination Ephemerides
Andrew Ellis
Claudia Petretti

Photographs
Jacques Faujour

on the cover:
J & J / Balthazar Burkhard
Venice and La Mariée
mise à nu par ses célibataires, même

Project for the Catalogue and
the Ephemerides by
Jennifer Gough-Cooper
Jacques Caumont
with the collaboration of
Eleanor Apter
Claude Rameil
Naomi Sawelson-Gorse
Assistant
Brigitta Cladders

frontispiece
Gisèle Freund
Marcel Duchamp, 1939

Computer-Interactive
Didactic Program
IBM SEMEA

Programs by Angelo Cerizza of Cleis S.r.l.,
produced by Seltering S.p.A.

Lenders

Museums

Basel, Kunstmuseum

Bruxelles, Musées Royaux des Beaux-Arts de Belgique

Chicago, The Art Institute

Claremont, The Francis Bacon Library

Halle, Staatliche Galerie Moritzburg

Houston, The Menil Collection

London, The Tate Gallery

Los Angeles, The Museum of Contemporary Art

Montauban, Musée Ingres

New Haven, Yale University Art Gallery

New York, The S.R. Guggenheim Museum

New York, The Museum of Modern Art

Paris, Bibliothèque Littéraire Jacques Doucet

Paris, Bibliothèque Nationale, Département des Manuscripts

Paris, Musée nationale d'art moderne, Centre Georges Pompidou

Philadelphia, The Philadelphia Museum of Art

Rouen, Bibliothèque Municipale

Sarasota, John and Mable Ringling Museum of Art

Stockholm, Moderna Museet

Stuttgart, Graphische Sammlung Staatsgalerie

Toyama, The Museum of Modern Art

Venice, Peggy Guggenheim Collection

Vienna, Graphische Sammlung Albertina

Wilmington, Delaware Art Museum

Private Collections

Bologna, Dino Gavina Collection

Geneva, Editions Claude Givaudan

Gstaad, Georges Marci Bianchi Collection

Heimhausen, Ursula and Klaus-Peter Bergmann Collection

Los Angeles, Robert Shapazian Collection

Milan, Bruno Alfieri Collection

Milan, Angelo Calmarini Collection

Milan, Archivio Ugo Mulas Collection

Milan, Arturo Schwarz Collection

New York, Sarah Goodwin Austin Collection

New York, Timothy Baum Collection

New York, Arne H. Ekstrom Collection

New York, Carroll Janis Collection

New York, Francis M. Naumann Collection

New York, Michael Senft Collection

Paris, Jean-Jacques Lebel Collection

Rome, Gianfranco Baruchello Collection

Tokyo, Galleria Tokoro

Venice, Renato Cardazzo Collection

Venice, Attilio Codognato Collection

Warelwast, Académie de Muséologie Evocatoire Collection

Alexina Duchamp Collection

Richard Hamilton Collection

Jedermann Collection

Patricia and Frank Kolodny Collection

André Raffray Collection

Dina Vierny Collection

Elizabeth S. Wrigley Collection

and others who wished to remain anonimous

"The Blind Lottery of Reputation"
or the Duchamp Effect

Pontus Hulten

The history of the appreciation of Marcel Duchamp's work has little in common with what has happened to the work of other artists of his generation. In the years just before and during the First World War, Duchamp was known in Paris and New York as an outstanding innovator; in fact he was world-famous before he was thirty years old. During the years that followed Duchamp continued to develop his work in an entirely logical manner, but the situation around him changed. It has been said that a couple of unfortunate accidents before the Second World War could have eliminated his work from art history and that, as a consequence, nothing would be known about it today. This is an exaggeration, no doubt, but it is still a sufficiently reasonable and well-founded conjecture not to be entirely ridiculous. If one considers that Vermeer van Delft was ignored by art historians for 200 years, this is not such an unlikely fate to befall an artist. Nonetheless, Duchamp seems to have foreseen the danger that his work might have been forgotten fairly early on. In the mid-1930s he started to arrange for a large portion of his work to be held in the Arensberg Collection; in 1934 he published the *Boîte Verte*, thus providing the basis for a proper understanding of his *magnum opus* the Large Glass. In 1936 Duchamp started the project for a "portable museum" of his work, the *Boîte-en-Valise*, which contained excellent reproductions of all the most important works he had produced until then.

In the presentation of the box – the "layout" – he gave some useful hints as to how the works should be observed and how they were related to each other.

One of the reasons why the art world soon lost interest in Duchamp was his aversion to the one-off, handmade, saleable object, such as the painting and the sculpture, which he stopped producing early on. The art world was so preoccupied with this kind of object that, in its eyes, Duchamp's refusal was tantamount to his having stopped working. Even his passion for chess permitted those envious of his freedom to say that he had abandoned art…

For somebody who decided not to repeat himself and to use a new idea only once, Duchamp's *œuvre* is immense, comprising more than 200 major pieces.

When in 1934 André Breton declared, in his usual provocative manner, that painting still needed to find its Gutenberg, it is a safe guess that a previous discussion with Duchamp lay behind his statement. It can also be assumed that the same thought expressed by Duchamp would have been formulated in a much more complex form. In fact, he expressed the need for art to liberate itself from the convention of the handmade marketable object in several different ways: by transforming his images into magazine covers, a cheque (for a dentist), shares (for a company devoted to playing roulette) and in 1935, in perhaps the most convincing way, the *Rotoreliefs*, which were virtual sculptures, visual disks to be "played" on a standard gramophone. They were sold for 15 francs in sets of six. It was characteristic of Duchamp that the answer to an important question lay not only in his abundant writings, but also in a related work, an image or a project. The writings, the "notes" are preparations for the image. The beauty of the total process is very stimulating.

There is immense pleasure to be derived from the contemplation of the different steps of these proceedings, which allow us to see how an important question is dealt with: seriously, elegantly and with great precision.

In the world we are living in today there is an intense escalation of the use of the image. It is a cause for satisfaction that, thanks to Duchamp, the question of reproduction became a matter for serious debate before the trivialization and mechanization that we encounter today.

As late as the 1940s, very few art historians occupied themselves with the history of the art of the twentieth century. It was actually forbidden in most universities. Books about "Modern Art" were usually written by artists, such as the hefty *Vision in Motion* by Moholy-Nagy, published posthumously in Chicago in 1947 or the Dada anthology *Dada Poets and Painters* by Robert Motherwell, published in New York in 1957. For this reason there was often a certain amount of partiality – even ill-feeling – in the presentation, reflecting conflicts between groups and schools, such as the one between Constructivism and Surrealism.

The rumour that Duchamp had stopped working, that he had left the Large Glass unfinished and that he was now devoting himself to chess made him easy prey for the malicious attacks of envious fellow artist-writers. One of the nastiest remarks came from Moholy-Nagy in *Vision in Motion*, where he reproduced the Green Box spread out on a table with the caption "Book (portfolio)", and claimed that Duchamp had been asked to publish his life's work and then emptied the contents of his desk into a cardboard box and had it reproduced, leaving the reader to try to make sense of the mess.

But such remarks merely whetted young people's curiosity. Marcel Duchamp's work became known by a new generation in the immediate postwar period, even in the more far-flung parts of Europe. That he belonged to the same family as Jacques Villon and Raymond Duchamp-Villon was very confusing for some academically biased professors preoccupied with psychological theories. One of them told his students that the reason for the "aggressiveness" of Duchamp's work was that he had a terrible inferiority complex with regard to his brother Jacques Villon. To fully understand this strange theory one must be aware that at that time Jacques Villon was much better known than Marcel. In the same vein, Cubism was explained as being the result of the experience of Georges Braque and Fernand Léger in the war, painting camouflage patterns on tanks and guns.

If one compares the vicissitudes of the appreciation of Duchamp's work with the history of the century in general, it is interesting to notice that the ups and downs seem to coincide. When his work was understood and appreciated things were going well for the rest of humanity; when the twentieth century was going through one of its bad moments, his work was spurned. The reason why Guillaume Apollinaire included Duchamp in his book *Les Peintres Cubistes* (1912) has been the subject of frequent speculation. Duchamp was then twenty-five years old and Apollinaire had probably seen only a few fairly insignificant works by him. When Apollinaire finished the first version of his text, Duchamp was not in Paris but in Munich and could, therefore, not have himself shown him the *Nude Descending a Staircase*, which had been refused by Gleizes and Metzinger for the Salon des Indépendants in March of the same year. One might think that Apollinaire's tremendous curiosity for anything new would be enough to explain his interest in Duchamp. The real reason is probably that Francis Picabia had asked Apollinaire to include Duchamp in his book – and Picabia's wish carried some weight because he helped to finance its publication.

What exactly happened between 8 October, when Apollinaire radically revised his text, and 10–11 October, when Duchamp came back to Paris from Munich, the opening of the Section d'Or exhibition on 10 October and the trip to the Jura that Apollinaire, Picabia and Duchamp went on between 20 and 26 October? It has not yet been clarified. It is certain that, in the end, Apollinaire gave Duchamp pride of place in the book. He removed some woolly criticism from the printer's proofs, and cast Duchamp in the role of the young herald of the great art of the future.

This became the concluding sentence in the new version of the book, and it has tremendous power: *Il sera peut-être réservé à un artiste aussi dégagé de préoccupations esthétiques, aussi préoccupé d'énergie que Marcel Duchamp, de réconcilier l'Art et le Peuple.*

This rather grandiose affirmation has sometimes been regarded as one of Apollinaire's more journalistic pronouncements, but now, at the end of the century, one could also interpret it in a quite literal sense. It then becomes an extremely perceptive statement.

"L'artiste ne sait pas ce qu'il fait. Et j'insiste là-dessus parce que les artists n'aiment pas que l'on dise ça."

When he made this statement in 1960, was Marcel Duchamp thinking about the genesis of his "readymade", his most significant contribution to history? What ever the case, it would be difficult to find a better example than this genesis to illustrate his assertion.

Let us try to reconstruct the history of the birth of the concept of the "readymade." Duchamp answered a related question when he commented that, when he turned the Bicycle Wheel, 1913 (the first work in this group), it reminded him of a fire in an open hearth. He had moved from the countryside to Paris, and missed the flames of an open fire. While this idea of replacing the flames is clearly not the underlying reason for the creation of the piece, what more beautiful and poetic an answer could one find?

The idea of collage work, introduced by Pablo Picasso and Georges Braque the year before (1912), must have interested Duchamp profoundly, although he never produced a Cubist-type collage himself. In a Cubist collage, a fragment of everyday reality – such as a cutting from a newspaper – is taken from among the materials in the studio and introduced into the painting as an integral part. This transfer intimates that the space of the painting and that of the studio are one and the same. The inverted Cubist perspective had already established that "picture space" lay within the space of the studio by developing it in front of the painting and not, as with Renaissance perspective, into the more abstract space behind the painted surface of the canvas. The extension of the picture space into the room, into the artist's studio, seemed less illusory, more "truthful".

As the collage idea became more fully understood and developed, everyday objects became part of the world created by the artist. This evolution is amply testified in the chronicles of art history. It would therefore seem that Duchamp's Bicycle Wheel was the necessary corollary to the collage. However, the issue was so deep and involved that it took over fifty years to be fully grasped. As late as 1954, when I asked Marcel Duchamp about the date of the Bicycle Wheel, he hesitated to call it a readymade.

It was not admitted definitively to the category until the early 1960s. The process was a gigantic, Herculean adventure.

In 1954 I wrote to Duchamp asking him, among other things, whether an object must necessarily be shown publicly to qualify as a readymade, or whether it is a readymade even if it never leaves the studio. He omitted to reply to this particular question – probably because I had not sufficiently appreciated the notion of the studio as a special space, much as the studio of the Cubist painter coincided with the space of the collaged object. It goes without saying that, if you have a rack for drying bottles in your wine cellar, it cannot be considered a readymade. It only becomes one when it is brought into the studio. In fact, when Duchamp published photographs of the readymades in the *Boîte -en-Valise*, they were clearly situated in the artist's studio. In conclusion, one might say that the Bicycle Wheel on the kitchen stool is an intermediate, transitory kind of object: a collage-sculpture-readymade. In answer to the question put to him in 1954 as to whether the bicycle wheel was the first readymade, Duchamp significantly replied: "not even Ready made 1913."

It is also interesting to note that Marcel Duchamp's great friend Constantin Brancusi was meanwhile struggling with a problem of a similar nature, namely, the sculpture and its base, its support. Shortly after, not later than 1916, Brancusi was ready to present the first of his Endless Columns, a form of sculpture which did not require a base. The Bicycle Wheel and the Endless Column would become two of the most influential creations of the century, but only in the last fifty years has their importance been fully appreciated.

Gradually, the concept of the man-made object becoming a work of art because it has been selected by the artist began to establish itself, and the following year (1914) Duchamp designated the first official readymade: a *porte-bouteille*, or *égouttoir*, a *sèche-bouteille*, that is, a common bottle rack.

Just how the idea made its way is, of course, the big question. When asked, Duchamp replied: "C'est une chose beaucoup plus profonde que l'inconscient, si vous voulez!"

Marcel Duchamp went to New York in 1915 and it was from there that the readymade idea got its definition and that he used the term for the first time. He wrote to his sister Suzanne in Paris on 15 January 1916 and asked her to go to his studio in Rue Saint-Hippolyte, where she would find a bicycle wheel and a *sèche-bouteille* or bottle rack. He asked her to inscribe certain words and sign the *sèche-bouteille*, and made her a gift of it.

The first two parts of the letter turned up in 1984, but the third part, in which he defines what she was to inscribe, has unfortunately been lost.

It is, however, hard to believe that among the literature on each of the readymades, no mention was made of the fact that in French this object is also called an *égouttoir*, meaning, approximately, a "de-dropper" (*goutter* in French means "to drop"), and *goût*, meaning "taste", has almost the same sound. Hence *égouttoir* could mean "the removal of taste", good or bad, from art. The first two readymades were lost when Marcel Duchamp's studio in Rue Saint-Hippolyte was cleared out.

At twenty-nine years of age, when he wrote his letter to his sister, Duchamp established a high point in the art history of our century. He was already a great cultural hero in several different ways. He was one of the most famous artists of his time, largely because of just one work, Nude

Descending a Staircase. He had made his first experiments with chance, *3 Stoppages Etalon*, which would have a seminal influence on the future evolution of art, and he had defined, through a long, conscious mental process which he considered much more profound than the subconscious, the notion of the *readymade*, an invention that was to become one of the most important elements in art fifty years later.

Duchamp wrote to his sister from New York. The difference in the artistic climate between Paris and New York, and the change of environment in a more general sense, had accelerated the definition of the idea of the readymade. The first years in New York, 1915 to 1918, were the greatest period in Duchamp's early moments of glory and influence. A combination of intuition and the ability to make the right decision at the right time brought him to what was, for a young artist, the most interesting city in the world at that moment. America was not yet at war. Duchamp was exempt from military service. The artistic and intellectual circles of New York received him as a hero and as the great inventor that he was, perhaps without realizing how well-earned and how fitting were the honours they showered on him.

The concept of the readymades was defined parallel to the work on the Large Glass. In 1918 Duchamp continued with the readymades in the shape of their shadows on his last oil painting *Tu m'*.

In the early1920s two distinct movements became discernible in the new art, one of which was Surrealism in Paris. Former Dadaist painters and poets were now grouping themselves in an increasingly militant manner around André Breton, and at the same time becoming more and more involved in the political infighting among the various revolutionary groups. Duchamp had strong affinities with these painters and poets and maintained a close bond with André Breton throughout his life. He was never a member of the Surrealist group or involved in their political activities, but served as a *générateur-arbitre*, a "generator judge", accepted and respected by its different members, especially when it came to organizing public exhibitions and other events.

The other leading movement that took shape in the early 1920s was Abstract art, which developed from Synthetic Cubism and the great Russian experience, the prime movers of which had been Kasimir Malevich and Vladimir Tatlin. Piet Mondrian became the leading figure of this movement, which formed itself into such groups as Abstraction-Création and Cercle et Carré, although it then became involved in increasingly academic discussions.

As can be seen from the short monographs that he wrote about a large number of artists, including Mondrian, for the catalogue of the Société Anonyme Collection, Duchamp was very well-disposed to Mondrian's art and that of certain others among his followers. Only later, when Duchamp came to Paris in 1954, did he shock the second generation of artists working in this Abstract art movement by talking about *un art rétinien*, retinal art, art concerned only with the eye, as opposed to *cervellité, cosa mentale* or "grey matter", meaning art relating to the total emotional and intellectual sphere of man.

Thus Duchamp felt no strong affinities with the two leading movements in the new art that he saw around him in the early 1920s. Most of the Surrealist work was probably deemed too shallow, decorative, morbid and gratuitous. He maintained a certain degree of interest, but remained detached. Was he disenchanted? In 1923 he had already declared the Large Glass "definitively unfinished". Through his rejection of the unique art object he held himself aloof from the central preoccupation of both the Surrealists and the "abstract" painters and sculptors. Duchamp's main interest was focused on his multiples and different kinds of publications; pictorial art was thus about to "find its Gutenberg". Duchamp also devoted more time to chess and became a member of the French national chess team in 1924.

In the 1930s Duchamp's work began to be neglected and even forgotten. The older generation sometimes demonstrated their resentment, like Pablo Picasso in his conversations with André Malraux, or Moholy-Nagy in his malicious remarks about the Green Box.

By and large, during the Second World War all creative artistic activity in Europe ceased, while in the Fascist and Communist countries, avant-garde art had been banned from 1933 onwards. Only in the late 1940s did the creativity and curiosity that had reigned in prewar days begin to appear again. But the real change did not occur until the latter part of the 1950s.

In the United States, and especially in New York, things were different. Artistic activity was not curtailed by the war. On the contrary, the war years were one of the most productive periods of American art. Duchamp came back to New York from Europe in 1942. The first book announcing a new interest in his work was published by Roberto Matta in New York in 1944. It was called *Duchamp's Glass. An Analytical Reflection*, and contained, reproduced at the end, a painting by Matta from the year before, entitled *The Bachelors Twenty Years After*.

It is very possible that the intricate play of perspective in the Large Glass contributed to Matta's inventive use of perspective and his conception of space. Not only is there bold use of perspective in the lower part of the Glass, where there are two central perspective viewpoints, one "old", one "new", but, and this is more important, the transparency of the picture creates a new kind of spatial concept that Matta explored in his work. In his painting reproduced in the book, and also later, he used a notion of space that is based neither on Cubist principles nor on Renaissance perspective. In fact, it is very similar to the highly ambivalent nebulous yet dynamic space structure one can find in a photograph of the Large Glass.

The spatial concept develops in front of and behind the painting's surface, very much like the space in the photographs of Miss Dreier's library, where the Large Glass was then installed. There are three photographs of the library in his book. Matta's canvas surface is equivalent to the surface of the Glass. Imaginary space is developed in front as well as behind. The surface, the painted surface, becomes the factor that holds the different spatial concepts together. "Painting – glass – mirror –these are the three substances in dynamic interrelation with the final image of the Glass. While we gaze upon the bride – there appears through the glass the image of the room wherein we stand and on the radiation of the mirror design lives the image of our own body," Matta writes in his book.

Matta was to work with this kind of spatial concept and turn it into a force that would deeply impress the other painters in New York, especially Jackson Pollock. It is moving that Matta felt the need to document his experience of the photographs of the Large Glass. Others like Mark Tobey would also use this kind of space in paintings from about the same time (for example: *The Void Devouring the Gadget Era*, 1942).

This way of dealing with space has not been given a name, but it would be tempting to call it "American space", partly because it is unlimited and undefined. This is the kind of space that

Jackson Pollock would later work with in his large drip paintings. It was the space that the American Expressionist painters would subsequently explore.

What especially attracted young people in the 1940s and the 1950s to Duchamp's work was its precision and its elegance. Second-generation Surrealism and second-generation Abstract art weighed heavily on the times, with their strong flavour of rehashed ideas.

As seen in the vigorously creative surroundings of the work of the Dada painters and poets, Duchamp's work had a special freshness that put it in a category of its own, especially because it was evident that he later kept well away from the products of the clumsily macabre Surrealists.

The first experience of handling the pieces of paper of the Green Box in a library (in the Bibliothèque Jacques Doucet, Bibliothèque Sainte-Geneviève) was, for someone who had barely heard about it, an astonishing experience, so extraordinary that the next day the reader had to come back with a friend who could testify that the experience had not been a dream.

One of the first of the tributes paid to Duchamp by the generation that was thirty years old in 1955, the generation of Jean Tinguely, Robert Rauschenberg and Jasper Johns, came in the form of the spring edition of the biannual magazine *Blandaren* (Mixer). It was published in 1954 in Stockholm as a cardboard box containing about forty printed items of different sizes "and four pocket films and some candy" (a toothbrush made out of black liquorice and white sugar). The Green Box was clearly the inspiration. In the Mixer box were original "spontaneous" paintings on paper, ironic remarks concerning American Abstract Expressionism and some of the first projects for Pop Art objects.

Over the years young artists would lift ideas from Duchamp with impunity, for the simple reason that his work was so little known. But this plagiarism became so frequent that eventually Duchamp had to be recognized as the originator of a very large part of the new European and American art.

An ultimately rather sterile attempt to interpret the Large Glass, based on its relation to the work of Kafka and on alchemistic terminology and concepts started in 1954 and continued for some time in the circles close to Surrealism. Duchamp did not participate in this debate, which in the end did not enrich its subject but which, nevertheless, focused much new attention on the Large Glass and its author's work in general. Another debate, also rather pointless, concerning Duchamp's relation to his family, did not contribute in a significant way to the understanding of his art and took place without any comment from the artist.

The publication of a new box entitled *Eau et Gaz à tous les étages*, 1959, showed that his creative spirit was far from exhausted.

In the 1960s interest in Duchamp's work grew tremendously, partly because of replicas of the Large Glass that became available in Europe, starting with the copy in Stockholm, made in 1961.

In the 1970s and 1980s the importance of Duchamp's work continued to grow. The great richness of the work, which could now be seen in its totality, became even more apparent.

As this century draws to a close, it is amusing and satisfying to observe that Duchamp's role has won universal recognition. If, in 1953, somebody had said that forty years later his work would be considered more important than Picasso's, that person would have been looked on as a madman. *Et pourtant...*

19

Duchamp's Presence

Luciano Berio

Marcel Duchamp: I have always thought that the unpredictable, ironic, anecdotal and restive spectacle of his poetics (a word Duchamp himself undoubtedly shied from, being an ideologue of chance and chess) was a foil for one of the most complex, headstrong, contradictory and significant personalities of the century. His laborious and inquisitorial presence among us is never at rest, and he continues to inhabit our consciousness of the sorrounding world, conditioning the way we observe daily "things".

The temptation to transfer the "Duchamp experience" to music has always been strong, but it is not that easy, nor, to my mind, is it conceptually productive. The season of *Musique Concrète* which evolved in Paris during the early postwar years under Pierre Schaeffer, who adopted a rather futuristic line in his transformation of acoustic scraps of concrete experiences, to some extent echoes the way in which Duchamp snatched standard objects from their context.

But the parallels were very slight, as the objects and sound anecdotes of Pierre Schaeffer have nothing in common with the essential dimension of Duchamp, which is composed of analytical passion, geometric obsession and cynical indifference to common sense. Only Marcel Duchamp, despite his being alien to all forms of transcendence, could claim to want "something in which the eye and the hand no longer count at all". For other eyes and in other hands such an utterance could easily have become a kind of epistemological parody. With Duchamp, however, it was essentially a declaration of his estrangement from the "work of art" as such, and a fleeting judgment on the impermanence of artistic endeavours.

Music of this century (music which requires no pigeonholing or cumbersome adjectives) has its fair share of unpredictable, ironic and unsettled personalities, but no one remotely comparable to Duchamp. Nor would it make sense if there were. Such parallels are ruled out by the intrinsically more meditative and slower processes of the musical experience, which tend above all to express and communicate themselves. Even when musical works seem to open up themselves to the outside (no longer aiming to relate and comment themselves alone) it is obvious that they can never supply concrete or metaphorical external references such as virgins or brides, chessplayers, industrial scrap, valises, bicycle wheels, Mona Lisas or urinals.

If he so wished, a composer was in a position to quote concrete examples, external to his creative world, taken from the entire history of music – but that is another thing altogether.

From the very outset, Marcel Duchamp never aimed to describe objects, to relate or comment on painting, nor even comment on his our unpredictable and highly zigzagging personal developments. In defiance of art, of the aura and the sacredness of the "work of art", Duchamp busied himself instead with geometrizing, anaesthetizing and frequently exasperating the latent conflicts between objects (in inverted commas), trying to desecrate the relationship between the eye, the hand and the mind. This is why he had no patience for the appeal and confort of *style* which he felt tantamount to *market* and induced the creator to repeat himself endlessly, doing what had become easy to him (sometimes at the cost of his life, as in Rothko's case). And this is why, a deconstructionist before his time, Duchamp insisted that in the long run it was the observer who made the picture, and that what really mattered – the idea and the links between ideas – should fit snugly into a suitcase: hence the *Boîte-en-Valise*.

It has frequently been voiced that John Cage was Duchamp's musical *alter ego*. True, they saw each other often and were close friends but, all things considered, apart from their inevitable and reciprocal intellectual attraction and apart from the fact that (with a pinch of anti-fetishistic ideological acrobatics) a "prepared" Steinway might be assimilated with the idea of Duchamp's bearded *Mona Lisa*, I think they shared above all a dialectic of semantic silence and of non-doing. What they refused to do often took on as much significance as what they actually did. It was a kind of very present absence, which in other creative minds has often been responsible for opportunistic stylistic strategies. Without going into the innumerable details of the individual creative paths of Duchamp and Cage, what springs to mind is their rejection of the notion of art, with all its aesthetic implications. I remember John Cage in the 1950s at the Studio di Fonologia Musicale in Milan, busy working at *Fontana Mix* (a sort of acoustic *Boîte-en-Valise*). In mixing the sound results of his rigorous aleatory operations, Cage refused to impose an overall dynamic shape to the piece, declaring that it was "too artistic".

The great feats of musical exploration, from Monteverdi to Schönberg and on to the present day, have generally been achieved under the protective umbrella of words sung (or almost sung) that, however complex was the musical process, guaranteed a meaning of some kind. Duchamp likewise, when he strayed into the somewhat uncharted realm of his Readymades, made use of words – in the titles of his works, of course – as did thousands of painters and sculptors both before and after him. But the function of the titles in Duchamp's work is a fairly complex and intriguing matter. They are not used as "lifesavers", to assure some kind of meaning and, obviously, they do not perform the elementary function of giving names to things. Nor, in a world that is not too unanimous and overcharged with merchandising, do they particularly upset the stock vocabulary of cultural codes and artistic genres (*Annunciation*, *Sonata II*, *Still-life*, *Symphony VII*, *Untitled*, *Composition*, and so on). I think that a short history of titles in visual arts has yet to be written. If such as thing existed, Duchamp would occupy a place of honour. His titles sometimes have a vaguely literary bent, such as Valise = *Sélavy* = *c'est la vie*. In other cases they are witty captions, as in *L.H.O.O.Q.*, which runs "Elle (i.e., the Mona Lisa) a chaud au cul", which Duchamp himself translated as "She has a hot arse". The titles lack the customary emphasis, the tautology and invitation, so much so that one suspects that the work conceals some unfathomable mystery. But it is certain that Duchamp's astute and evasive *profondeur* is *partout et nulle part*. His modernity resides in the uncanny mobility of the relationship that he sets up between symbol and object: between a banal object which becomes a symbol and identifies with another symbol which, with no guarantee whatsoever, in turn evokes other objects and symbols. In this mechanism of prompts and cues, the creative input of the title is important. In fact Duchamp's titles could quite reasonably become the subject of a semiological study of communication, especially if touched by a vein of irony. The famous *Fountain*, for instance, one of the first installations in art history, triggers a labyrinth of conflicts. It is an *objet trouvé*, accurately chosen and re-chosen. In its new location on public display in a museum, it is no longer a receptacle. Instead, as its title implies, it emits liquid. To urinate in a exhibition is hardly practical, if not to say downright inconvenient. One runs less of a risk if instead one expresses one's disgust towards the art market with an icon, a residue of industrial production, however offensive it may be, which, signed by an authoritative name between inverted commas, no longer conserves its original function. Etcetera.

The links between the creative work and the *outside* are, in most cases, intuitive. It is maybe pointless, therefore, to insist in interpreting them. If Picasso had not hung his walls with those particular African masks, would he have thought of the *Demoiselles d'Avignon* as we know them today? To my mind, in Duchamp's case, the relationship between *outside* (a title, for instance) and *inside* (an object come upon even by chance, assimilated and transformed) has meaning only when it lends plurality, a mobile and open plurality to meaningful links. And, of course, when the object itself is already freighted with a not necessarily explicit meaning. In other hands, and to other eyes, those links can become fixed, and to some extent decline to the point that the conflicts fall away. Such is the case with Magritte's gastronomic Surrealism. If you take away the title, not much remains.

Every form of art that is forward-looking – and hence worthy of the utmost attention – speaks of the conflicts inherent to its creation, its processes and the components of which it is constituted, be they concrete or conceptual. Music too, and particularly music which strives to *reveal* something rather than just *represent* it, speaks implicitly of its inherent conflicts and its creation, its torments and structural passions. Beyond the relative incommunicability and specificity of these two diverse experiences, the work of Marcel Duchamp, with its tireless self-questioning about things, forms and concepts, is closer to music than perhaps even he imagined. But nothing can quash my doubt whether, had Duchamp had a closer experience of music, his work would have acquired a further dimension: it would have had to tackle other conflicts (between the real and the virtual?), of a decidedly less concrete and anecdotal nature, but perhaps loftier.

Duchamp's *œuvre* is an occasion somewhat healthly difficult to identify with, not only because it sidesteps sentimental banalization and the snares of rhetoric, but also because it never ceases to outspokenly declaim the thorny though unavoidable issue, the attractive though insoluble issue of our relationship with physical reality and with the ideas and the constantly evolving tools with which that reality is accessed and interpreted: the relationship between the concrete and the abstract.

On and about the exhibition

*Mélanges
d'évènements imagés plastiquement.*

25

Plastically imaged mixture
of events using notation
by or of Marcel Duchamp
and Rrose Sélavy

The detailed description of each work exhibited is to be found in the alphabetical list of works in the central pages of this volume.
In this list there is also a translation of the title of each work when appropriate and, in square brackets, the date of the main entry relating to it in the Ephemerides.

 Indicates those works which Duchamp reproduced in the Boîte-en-valise

 Indicates those works which Duchamp reproduced in the Green Box.

The date of each work is stated at the edge of each page.

The size of certain works is indicated in relation to the size of the illustration.

The position of a particular element in the Large Glass to which a work refers is indicated with a red dot on this small diagram of the Glass.

The illustration of the Large Glass may be unfolded for reference while the reader consults the catalogue.

Facsimiles of Duchamp's notes in the catalogue have been taken from the *La Mariée mise à nu par ses célibataires, même* (known as the Green Box), Edition Rrose Sélavy, Paris, 1934; *The Bride stripped bare by her Bachelors, even*, the typographic version by Richard Hamilton of the Green Box, translated by George Heard Hamilton, Percy Lund, Humphries and Co. Ltd London and George Wittenborn Inc., New York, 1960; *A l'infinitif*, Cordier & Ekstrom, New York 1966; *Marcel Duchamp, Notes*, published posthumously by the Centre National d'Art et de Culture Georges Pompidou, Paris 1980; and other manuscripts and interviews.

The diagram of the Large Glass by Jean Suquet is taken from *Le Grand Verre rêvé*, Edition Aubier, Paris.

J.C.

26

1. mètres étalon
(2. célibataires
((3. les "readymades"
(((4. Rrose Sélavy
((((5. le "Grand Verre". 5))))
mariée. 6)))
boîte-en-valise. 7))
étant donnés. 8)
maîtres étalon. 9

Can one make works
which are not works
of "art"?

Pat on faire des œuvres qui ne
soient pas 'd'art. "? —

28

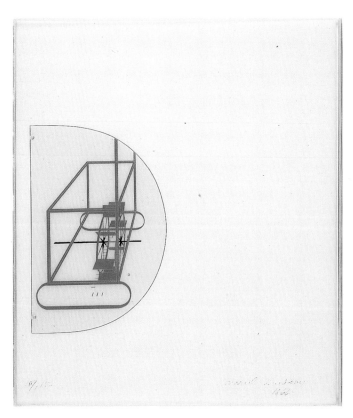

A l'infinitif

Il ne peut plus être question d'un
Beau plastique.

It can no longer be a
matter of a plastic Beauty

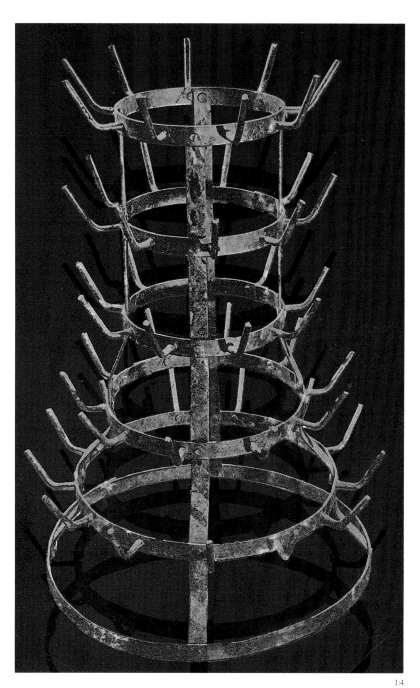

1:4

Egouttoir

The idea of contemplation
disappears completely.
Simply note that it was a
bottle-rack which changed
its destination.

1913

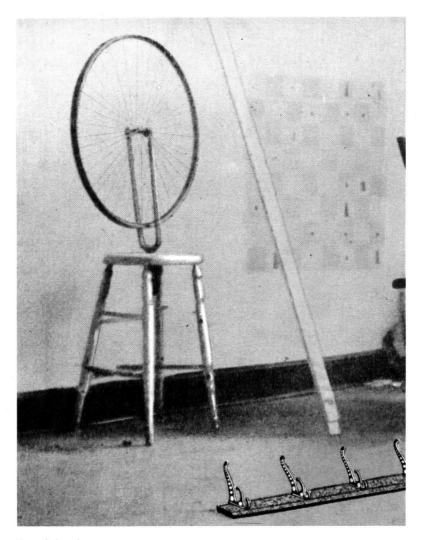

Roue de bicyclette

30

The statue in corset
whalebone travelling
on rails made
of calf's lights.

Raymond Roussel,
Impressions d'Afrique
1912

hinge

1 Mètres étalon and related works

3 Stoppages Etalon =
du hasard en conserve

1914.

3 Standard Stops =

_____ canned chance

1914.

l'Idée de la Fabrication

— Si un fil horizontal d'un mètre de longueur tombe droit d'un mètre de hauteur sur un plan horizontal en se déformant à son gré et donne une figure nouvelle de l'unité de longueur. —

the Idea of the Fabrication

_____

horizontal
——— If a thread one meter long falls
straight
from a height of one meter on to a horizontal plane

twisting as it pleases and creates

a new image of the unit of length. ———

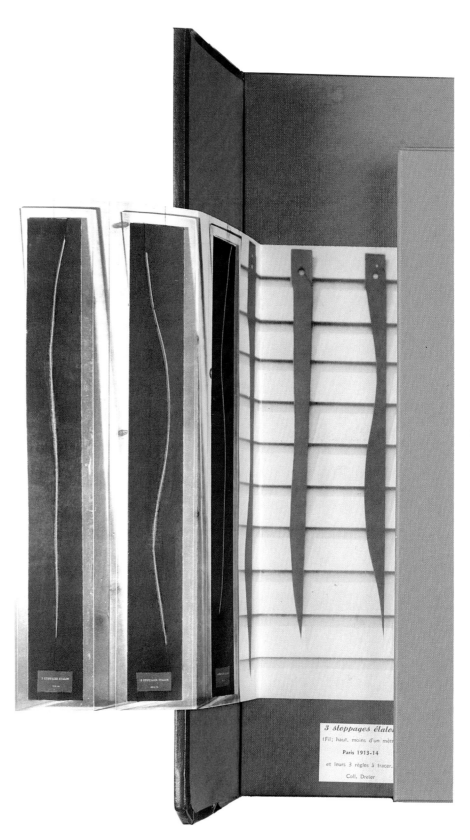

Le chef des 5 nus obtient peu à peu l'annexion de la route Jura-Paris

Le chef des 5 nus annexe à ses états, après une lutte
(idée de colonie)

The chief of the 5 nudes manages little by little the annexation of the Jura-Paris road.
The chief of the 5 nudes annexes to his estates, a battle (idea of colony)

Titre.

Le chef des 5 nus étend peu à peu son pouvoir sur la route Jura-Paris.

Il y a un peu équivoque: Ce chef semble, après avoir conquis les 5 nus, agrandi ses possessions; ce qui donne un sens faux au titre. (Les 5 nus et lui forment tribu à la conquête par la vitesse de cette route Jura-Paris)

Le chef des 5 nus peu à peu augmente son pouvoir sur la route Jura-Paris.

La route Jura-Paris, d'un côté, les 5 nus dont le chef, d'un autre côté, sont les deux termes de la collision. Cette collision est la raison d'être du tableau. Peindre 5 nus statiquement, me semble sans intérêt, pas plus d'ailleurs que de peindre la route Jura-Paris même en élevant l'interprétation picturale de cette entité à un état tout à fait dénué d'impressi. Donc l'intérêt du tableau résulte de la collision de ces 2 extrêmes, les 5 nus dont le chef et la route Jura-Paris. Le résultat de cette bataille sera la victoire peu à peu obtenue par les 5 nus sur la route Jura-Paris.

34

1912

Title.
The chief of the 5 nudes extends little by little his power over the Jura-Paris road.
There is a little ambivalence: After having conquered the 5 nudes, this chief seems to enlarge his possessions, which gives a false meaning to the title. (He and the 5 nudes form a tribe for the conquest by speed of this Jura-Paris road) The chief of the 5 nudes increases little by little his power over the Jura-Paris road.

The Jura-Paris road, on one side, the 5 nudes one the chief, on another side, are the two terms of the collision. This collision is the raison d'être of the picture. To paint 5 nudes statically seems to me without interest, no more for that matter than to paint the Jura-Paris road even by raising the pictorial interpretation of this entity to a state entirely devoid of impressionism. Thus the interest in the picture results from the collision of these 2 extremes, the 5 nudes one the chief and the Jura-Paris road. The result of this battle will be the victory obtained little by little by the 5 nudes over the Jura-Paris road.

The village of Etival in the Jura. It was on his return from Etival to Paris, in October 1912, that Duchamp wrote the note: Jura-Paris road.

[handwritten note in French]

This headlight child could, graphically, be a comet, which would have its tail in front, this tail being an appendage of the headlight child appendage which absorbs by crushing (gold dust, graphically) this Jura-Paris road.

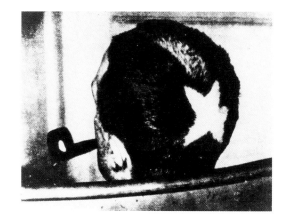

Duchamp with the comet haircut shaved by Georges de Zayas, c. 1919

Pictorial Translation - The 5 nudes, one the chief, will have to lose, in the picture, the character of multiplicity. They must be a machine of 5 hearts, an immobile machine of 5 hearts The chief, in this machine, could be indicated in the center and at the top, without appearing to be anything other than a more important gear-train (graphically).
This machine of 5 hearts will have to give birth to the headlight. This headlight will be the child-God, rather like the primitives' Jesus. He will be the divine blossoming of this machine-mother. In graphic form, I see him as pure machine compared to the more human machine-mother. He will have to be **radiant with glory**. And the graphic means to obtain this machine-child, will find their expression in the use of the purest metals for a construction based (as a construction) on the concept of an endless screw, (accessories of this endless screw. serving to unite this headlight child God, to his machine-mother, 5 nudes.

Traduction picturale.

Les 5 nus, dont le chef, devront perdre, dans le tableau, le caractère de multiplicité. Ils doivent être une machine à 5 cœurs, une machine immobile à 5 cœurs Le chef, dans cette machine, pourra être indiqué au centre ou au sommet, sans paraître autre chose qu'un rouage plus important (graphiquement).

Cette machine à 5 cœurs devra enfanter le phare.
Le phare sera l'enfant-Dieu, rappelant assez le Jésus des primitifs.
Il sera l'épanouissement divin de cette machine-mère.
Comme forme graphique, je le vois machine pure par rapport à la machine-mère, plus humaine. Il devra rayonner de gloire. Et les moyens graphiques pour obtenir cet enfant-machine, trouveront leur expression dans l'emploi des plus purs métaux servant à la construction basée (en tant que construction) sur l'idée qui se dégage d'une vis sans fin. (accessoires de cette vis sans fin, servant à unir ce phare enfant Dieu. à la mère machine. 5 nus.

1912

cet épanouissant

est l'image d'une voiture auto. qui monte une
côte à en 1ère vitesse. (la voiture désire de plus
en plus le haut de la montée, et tout en
accélérant lentement, comme fatiguée d'espoir,
elle répète par coups de moteur réguliers d'une
vitesse de plus en plus grande, jusqu'au ronflement
triomphal.

this blossoming
is the image of a motor car climbing a
slope in low gear. (The car wants more
and more to reach the top, and while
slowly accelerating, as if exhausted by hope,
the motor of the car turns over
faster and faster, until it roars
triumphantly.

37

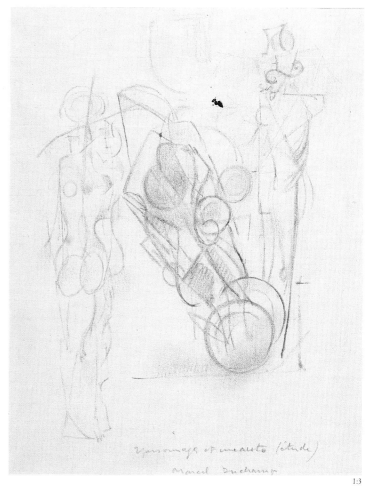

1:3

2 personnages et une auto

a kind of new musical alphabet

En haut de la mise à nu : petits canons lance-
bille (ou wagonnet).

At the top of the stripping-
bare: little marble-shooting
cannons (or small wagons).

La Mariée mise à nu par
ses célibataires, même.
Erratum musical

Mise à nu en forme de piano
accompagné des 3 fracas et des souvenirs
de jeunesse du gaz d'éclairage.

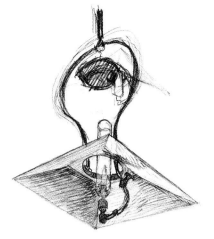

Stripped bare in piano form accompanied by the 3 crashes and the childhood memories of the illuminating gas.

"Each n° indicates a note; an ordinary piano contains about 89 notes; each n° is the number in order starting from the left.

Unfinishable; for a designated musical instrument (player piano, mechanical organs or other new instruments for which the virtuoso intermediary is suppressed); the order of succession is (to taste) interchangeable; the time which separates each Roman numeral will probably be constant (?) but it may vary from one performance to another; a very useless performance in any case.

An apparatus automatically, recording fragmented musical periods

Vase containing the 89 notes (or more: 1/4 tone) figures among n° on each ball.

Opening A letting the balls drop into a serie of little wagons B.C.D.E.F. etc

Wagons B, C, D, E, F, going at a variable speed, each one receiving one or several balls

When the vase is empty: the period in 89 notes (so many) is inscribed and can be performed by a designated instrument

another vase - another period - the result from the equivalence of the periods and their comparison a kind of new musical alphabet allowing model descriptions. (to be developed)."

La mariée mise à nu par ses célibataires mêmes ;
pour écarter le tout fait, en série du
tout trouvé — L'écart est une opération.

The Bride stripped bare by her bachelors even.

to separate the mass-produced readymade from the
readyfound—The separation is an operation.

40

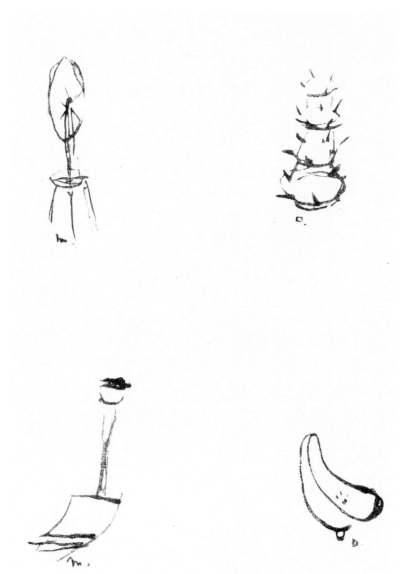

4 Ready-mades, 1964

Four Readymades

1:2

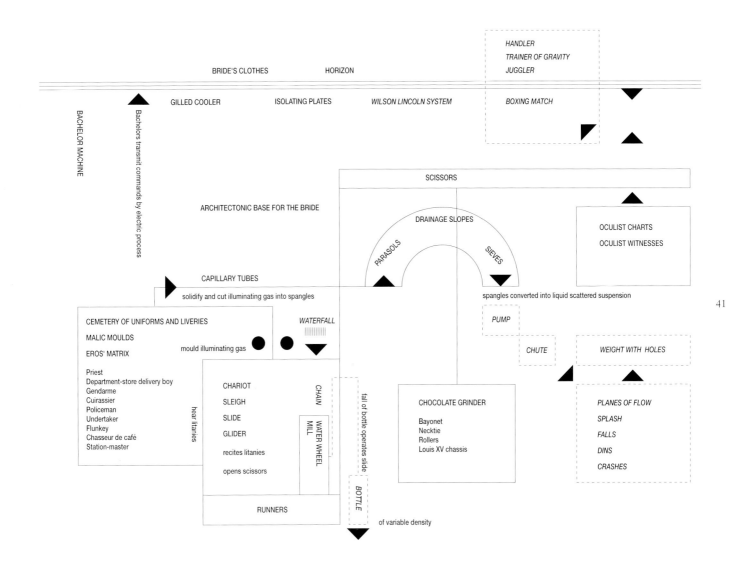

BRIDE'S CLOTHES   HORIZON

HANDLER
TRAINER OF GRAVITY
JUGGLER

GILLED COOLER   ISOLATING PLATES   *WILSON LINCOLN SYSTEM*   BOXING MATCH

BACHELOR MACHINE

Bachelors transmit commands by electric process

ARCHITECTONIC BASE FOR THE BRIDE

SCISSORS

DRAINAGE SLOPES

PARASOLS   SIEVES

OCULIST CHARTS
OCULIST WITNESSES

CAPILLARY TUBES

solidify and cut illuminating gas into spangles

spangles converted into liquid scattered suspension

41

CEMETERY OF UNIFORMS AND LIVERIES

MALIC MOULDS

EROS' MATRIX

mould illuminating gas

WATERFALL

PUMP

CHUTE   *WEIGHT WITH HOLES*

Priest
Department-store delivery boy
Gendarme
Cuirassier
Policeman
Undertaker
Flunkey
Chasseur de café
Station-master

hear litanies

CHARIOT

SLEIGH

SLIDE

GLIDER

recites litanies

opens scissors

CHAIN

WATER WHEEL
MILL

fall of bottle operates slide

CHOCOLATE GRINDER

Bayonet
Necktie
Rollers
Louis XV chassis

PLANES OF FLOW

SPLASH

FALLS

DINS

CRASHES

BOTTLE

RUNNERS

of variable density

from the diagram by
Richard Hamilton

Trituration of the
illuminating gas

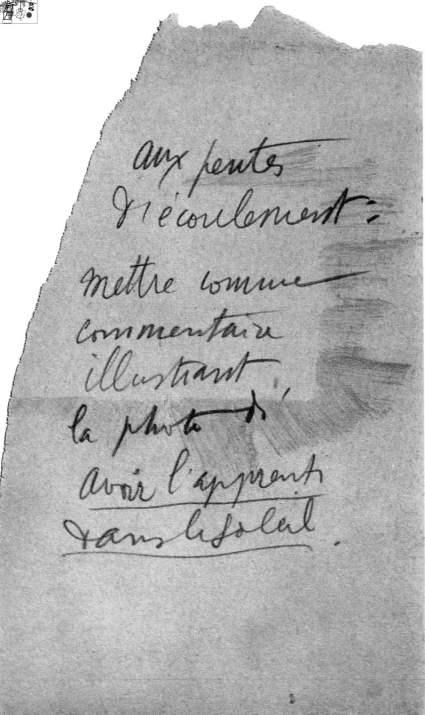

Boîte de 1914

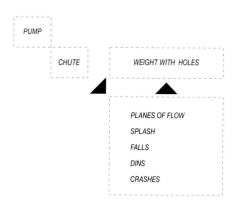

on the slopes of flow: put
like a comment illustrating
the photo of *having the
apprentice in the sun.*

42

1:3

Exposition Internationale
du Surréalisme
Paris 1938

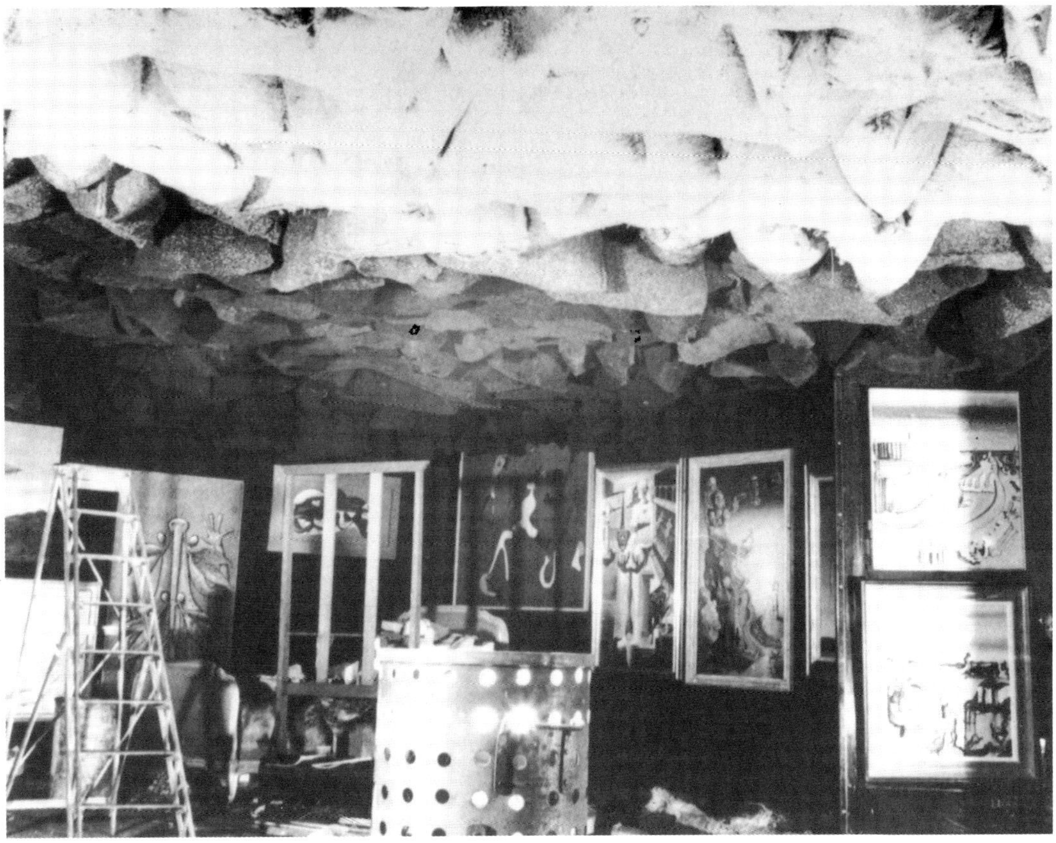

~~l'aiguille pouls doit avoir sa source dans le centre vie. de la mariée. (La mariée a un centre vie – les célibat. n'en ont pas. Ils vivent par le charbon ou autre matière première tirée non d'eux mais de leur non eux.~~

~~the pulse needle should have its source in the life center. of the
Bride. (The Bride has a life center—the bachelors have
not. They live on coal or other raw material
drawn not from them but from their not them.~~

Comparaison: [redacted] trouver le correspondant en peinture de la comparaison dans la littérature (comme ....)

Comparison: find what
corresponds in painting to
comparison in literature
(like...)

—Provisional color $=$ The malic forms. They are
provisionally painted with red lead while waiting for each
one to receive its color, like
croquet mallets.

Progress (improvement)   Given the illuminating gas.
~~Journey~~ of the illuminating gas up to the planes of flow

Malique moulds. (Malic(?))

By Eros' matrix, we understand the group
of ^{8} uniforms or hollow liveries
         receive the   which takes
destined to give to the illuminating gas 8 malic
forms (gendarme, cuirassier etc.)

The gas castings so obtained
would hear the litanies sung by
the chariot, refrain of the whole celibate machine,
but they will never be able to (pass beyond) (the Mask) $=$ They
would have been as if enveloped, alongside their
regrets, by a mirror reflecting back to them their
own complexity to the point of their being hallucinated rather
onanistically. (Cemetery of ^{8} uniforms or liveries)

Each of the 8 malic forms
is (built) above and below a common
horizontal
plane, the plane of sex cutting them at the point of sex.

(refer to figure)

      or   Each of the 8 malic forms is cut by an imaginary
horizontal plane at a point called the point of sex.

44

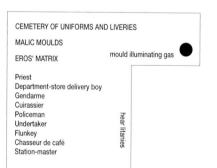

CEMETERY OF UNIFORMS AND LIVERIES

MALIC MOULDS

EROS' MATRIX   mould illuminating gas ●

Priest
Department-store delivery boy
Gendarme
Cuirassier
Policeman
Undertaker
Flunkey
Chasseur de café
Station-master

hear litanies

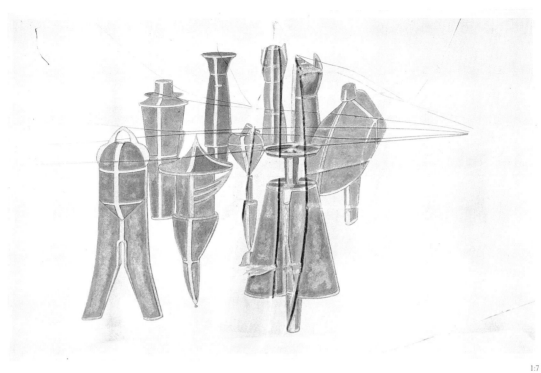

9 moules mâlic

matrices d'eros.

1:4

Cimetière des uniformes
et livrées, No. 2

The <u>principal forms</u> of the Bachelor Machine
are imperfect: rectangle, circle, parallelepiped,
symmetrical handle, demi-sphere = i.e.
they are mensurable (relation of their
dimensions among themselves. and relation of these
principal forms
to their destination in the Bachelor Machine)

addressing himself to me,
speaking to me personally,
said:
"It is probable that you
have no conception,
Panmuphle, writ-carrying
bailiff, of capillarity
Alfred Jarry, *Faustroll*
Book I, Chapter VI

pataphysic

Progress (improvement)

~~Journey~~ of the illuminating gas up to the planes of flow. (continued)

24

the capillary tubes

A { each malic form terminates at the head in

3 capillary tubes, (the 24 therefore) were supposed

to cut the gas in bits and would have led it

to disguise itself as 24 fine

solid needles so that they will become when reunited

2

once again, in the demi-siphons, a fog

made of a thousand spangles of frosty gas.

B ↓ At the head, [at the summit], of each malic mould

3 capillary tubes, (24 in all) to cut the gas

in bits, to cut the gas in long needles

(already) solid, since before becoming an explosive liquid,

solid

it takes the form of a fog of spangles of frosty gas, all

this by the phenomenon of <u>stretching in the unit of length</u>

(refer to figure)

When the 2 demi-siphons (letter in fig.) would have been filled

with the fog of spangles which

are lighter than air, the operation of

began

the liquefaction of the gas through the sieve and the horizontal filter:

each spangle of solid gas strives (in a kind of spangle

derby) to (pass) the holes of the sieve

with élan, reacting already to the suction of the pump.

▶ CAPILLARY TUBES

solidify and cut illuminating gas into spangles

Photographié en position perspective les 9 unités partant. du sommet de chaque moule . et allant se réunir sous. les tamis. (le r.ᵉ tamis.)

46

Photograph in perspective
position the 9 units going,
from the summit of each
mold, and reuniting under
the sieves. (the 1st sieve.)

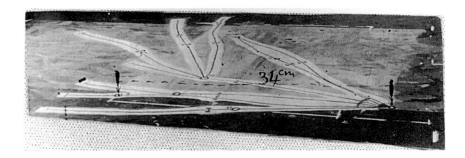

Roussel showed me the way

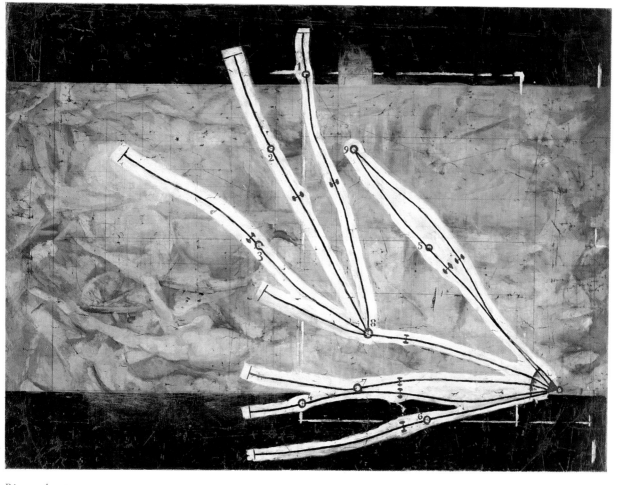

Réseaux des stoppages
étalon

Self-evident truths:

In a space, 2 straight lines intersecting determine a plane
or 2-dim'l continuum

In a space, 3 straight lines intersecting at a common point
determine a 3-dim'l space

In a plane, 3 straight lines intersecting do not determine
a space. Therefore in a space[4] lines intersecting
do not determine a continuum

Médiocrité

1913
1914

1:6

Broyeuse de chocolat, No. 1

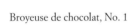

48

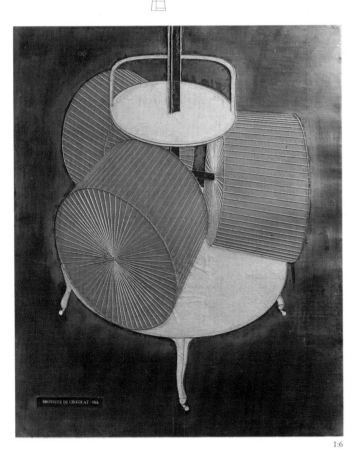

1:6

Broyeuse de chocolat, No. 2

Chocolate grinder with
three rollers in Gamelin's
window, Rue Beauvoisine,
Rouen

mach. Célibataire.

Broyeuse de chocolat

the Chocolate Grinder

is essentially composed . . .

} The chocolate of the rollers, (coming from one knows not where,) would deposit itself after grinding, as milk chocolate . . . . .

} (insert a letter referring to a diagram) with brilliant shimmering
The necktie would have been of aluminum foil stretched and stuck down, but the 3 rollers always turn beneath.

} the (Bayonet) (X) Helps to hold up the compression bar
and the large scissors and the isolating plates.

First-class article.

} The grinder is mounted on a Louis XV (nickeled) chassis.

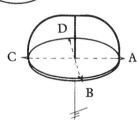

The necktie will owe its elegance to its thickness—

½ cm. or 1 ᶜᵐ at the most
resplendent
It will be brilliant above.

perhaps 4 points on the sides, A B C D.

very pointed (like all neckties)

[to be put in the text]

Description of the necktie:

1. resplendent in color

2. provided at the 4 corners with
   very sharp points (like all neckties.

49

"Le célibataire broie son chocolat lui même".

"The bachelor grinds his chocolate himself".

CHOCOLATE GRINDER

Bayonet
Necktie
Rollers
Louis XV chassis

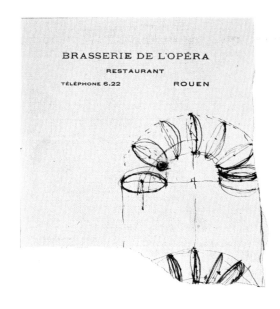

BRASSERIE DE L'OPÉRA
RESTAURANT
TÉLÉPHONE 6.22   ROUEN

sieves

For the in the glass—allow dust to

fall on this part a dust of 3 or 4 months

and wipe well around it in such a way that this dust

will be a kind of color (transparent pastel)

(Use of mica)

To be mentioned
the quality of
the other side of the dust
either as the name
of the metal or otherwise

Elever de la poussière

To raise dust

Also try to find several layers of transparent colors
(probably with varnish) one above the other. the
whole on glass.——

Doctor Faustroll was sixty-
three years old when he
was born in Circassia in
1898 (the 20th century was
(-2) years old).
So as not to embarrass the
populace, he drew on tiny
little gray boots, with even
layers of dust carefully
preserved on them, at great
expense, for many months
past.
Alfred Jarry, *Faustroll*,
Book I, Chapter II

Elevage de poussière,
photo Man Ray

DRAINAGE SLOPES
PARASOLS   SIEVES
spangles converted into liquid scattered suspension

pataphysic

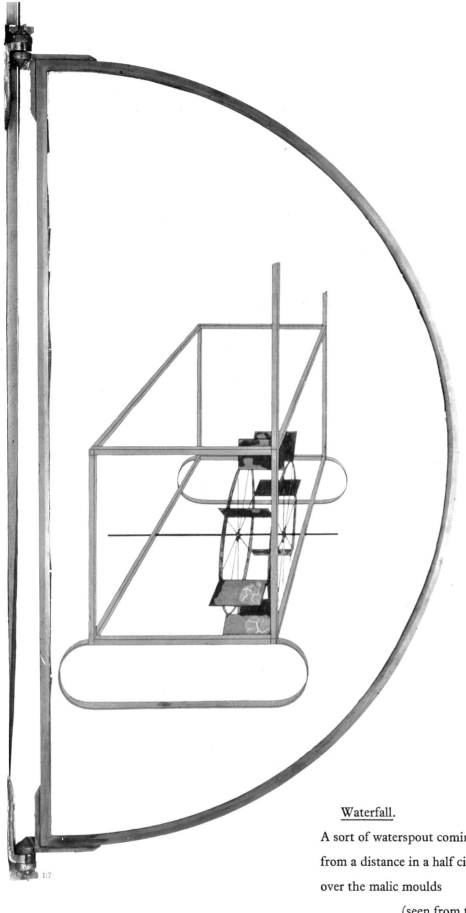

51

Water mill on the Crevon,
near Blainville

Waterfall.

A sort of waterspout coming

from a distance in a half circle

over the malic moulds

(seen from the side)

glider   moulds

Glissière contenant un
moulin à eau (en métaux
voisins)

1:7

A ≡ <u>axis</u> of the wheel <u>which</u> should drag the bottle of Benedictine.

A

52

Glissière (verso)

Chariot — Sleigh — Glider

The metal (or material)—of the chariot is
  <u>emancipated</u>. i.e.: that it has a weight
  but a force acting horizontally
  on the chariot does not have to support this
  weight (the <u>weight</u> of the metal does not <u>impede</u>
  a horizontal traction (to be developed)). The
  chariot is <u>emancipated horizontally</u>.

WATERFALL
|||||||||

CHARIOT
SLEIGH
SLIDE
GLIDER

recites litanies

opens scissors

CHAIN

WATER WHEEL MILL

RUNNERS

Chariot.

the litanies of the Chariot:

Slow life.
Vicious circle.
Onanism.
Horizontal.
Round trip
for the buffer.
Junk of life.
Cheap construction.
Tin, cords,
iron wire.
Eccentric wooden
pulleys.
Monotonous fly wheel.
Beer professor.
(to be entirely redone).

A   B

Yes but finally the fall of
bottles was replaced by an
imaginary waterfall

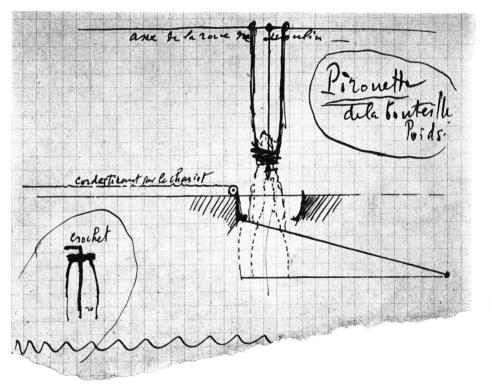

53

Chariot.

fall of bottle operates slide

BOTTLE

of variable density

Stained glass window in
the Benedictine Distillery,
Fécamp

Stéréoscopie à la main

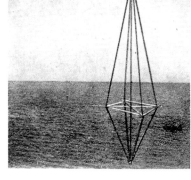

1918
1919

Optician's sign which belonged to Mary Reynolds, Rue Hallé

Tableau, l'oculiste —

Oculist's charts—

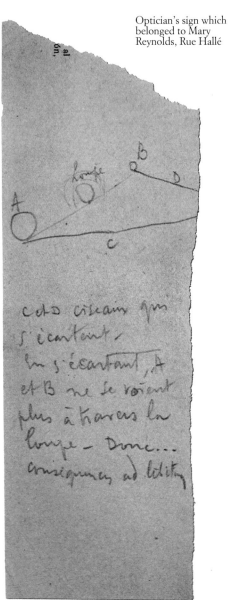

54

C and D scissors which open. In opening, A and B no longer see themselves through the magnifying glass - Therefore... consequences ad libitum

A regarder (l'autre côté du verre) d'un œil, de près, pendant presque une heure

AVKQIT.
avec acuité
R aère

OCULIST CHARTS
OCULIST WITNESSES

Comme fond, peut-être :
        une fête électrique rappelant les décors lumineux de
Magic City ou Luna Park, ou le Pier Pavilion à Herne Bay. — guirlandes
de lumières sur fond noir (ou fond de mer, bleu de Prusse et bistre)
Lampes à arc. — Feu d'artifice au figuré — En somme toile de
fond féerique (lointaine) sur laquelle se présente le ~~moin~~...
l'instrument agricole —

As background, perhaps:
An electric fete recalling
the decorative lighting of
Magic city or Luna Park,
or the Pier Pavilion at
Herne Bay - garlands of
lights against a black
background (or a
background of the sea.
Prussian blue and sepia)
Arc lights. - Figuratively a
fireworks - In short, a
magical (distant) back drop
in front of which is
presented... the agricultural
instrument -

, a Private Company un... ...
chased and improved by the local authority o.

GRAND PAVILION ILLUMINATED.
oto by   Fred. C. Palmer.
Grand Pier Pavilion was erected by the
... ... opened on the 3rd August
...don (Sir John

1 ⁰⁄₄864   Paris December 3ʳᵈ 1919

The Teeth's Loan & Trust Company, Consolidated
2 Wall Street.
New York.

Pay to the Order of Daniel Tzanck
One hundred fifteen and ⁿᵒ⁄₁₀₀   Dollars

$ 115. ⁰⁰⁄₁₀₀

Marcel Duchamp

55

ORIGIN

Chèque Tzanck

1:3

(effet argent)

Use ground glass behind
which one lays mat black
paper
(silvered effect)
(in the opticeries)

Buenos Aires, 1919

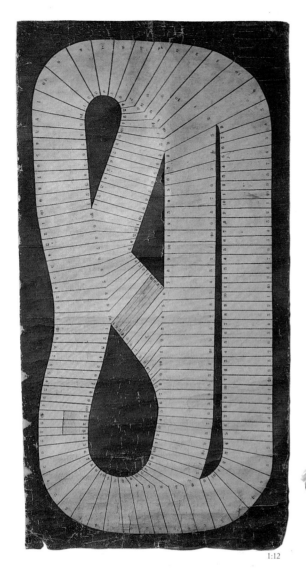

1:12

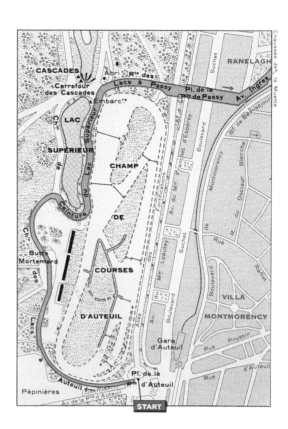

56

Gambit, one of the toy
horses from Marcel's stable

As in a Derby, the spangles pass through
the parasols A, C D.E F . . . B.

La convention du signe de la flèche produit une réaction infra mince sur le sens de déplacement accepté.

The convention of the
arrow sign produces an
infra thin reaction on the
sense of displacement
agreed to

1911

Coffee mill which
belonged to Mary Reynolds,
Rue Hallé

57

Moulin à café

1:1.5

1914
1918

Sculpture de voyage

58

Pharmacie

1:2

1941

... pliant, ... de voyage

Fania Marinoff

Poesia ed amore

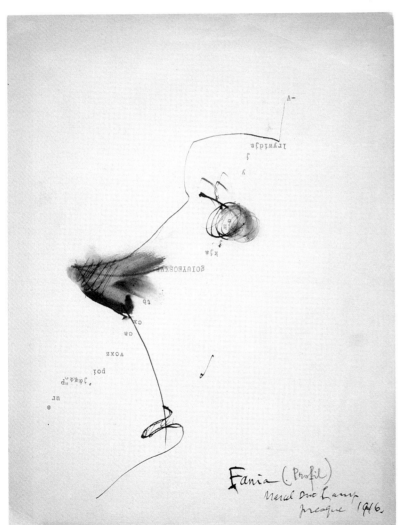

Fania (profil)

1:2

59

1915

60

The

If you come into ✦ linen, your time is thirsty because ✦ ink saw ~~some~~ wood intelligent enough to get giddiness from a sister. However, even it should be smilable to shut ✦ hair ~~of~~ which ✦ water writes always *meaning* plural, they have avoided ✦ frequency, mother in law; ✦ powder will take a chance; and ✦ road could try. But after somebody brought any multiplication as ~~soon~~ as ✦ stamp was out, a great many cords refused to go through. Around ✦ wire's people, who will be able to sweeten ✦ rug, ~~that is to say~~ ~~it means~~, why must every patents look for a wife? Pushing four dangers near ✦ listening-place, ✦ vacation had not dug absolutely nor this likeness has eaten.

remplacer chaque ✦ par le mot, the

THE SIMPLE ANAGRAMMATIC ACROSTIC   97

Page 280—

"i refer them also to that which plato said of his master socrates, whom he compared to the gallypots of apothecaries, which on the outside had apes and owls and Antiques, But CONtained within sovereign and precious liquors and confections; acknowledging that to an external report he was not without superficial levities and deformities, but was inwardly replenished with excellent virtues and powers."

Read the capitalised acrostic letters: BACON.

Page 280—

"but in the meantime i have no purpose to give allowance to some conditions and COurses Base ANd unworthy, wherein divers professors of learning have wronged themselves and gone too far;"

Read the capitalised acrostic letters: BACON.

Page 284—

"the echo answered . . . . the learning of the schoolmen to be utterly despised as barbarous. in sum, the whole INClination And Bent OF those times was rather towards copie"

Read the capitalised acrostic letters: I, F. BACON.

Page 285-286—

"laborious webs of learning which are extant in their books. for the wit and mind of man, if it work upon matter, which is the contemplation of the creatures of god, worketh according to the stuff, and is limited thereby; but if it work upon itself, as the spider worketh his web, then it is endless, ANd Brings Forth Indeed Cobwebs Of learning, admirable for the fineness of thread and work, but of no substance or profit."

Read the capitalised acrostic letters: I, F. BACON.

Page 286—

"upon every particular position or assertion to frame objections, and to those objections, solutions; . . . *verborum minutiis rerum frangit pondera* . . . . better for a man in a fair room to set up one great light, or Branching CANdle-

Extract from, *The Cryptography of Shakespeare*, by Walter C. Arensberg, Howard Bowen, Los Angeles 1922.

THIS SIDE OF CARD IS FOR ADDRESS

-toir. On manquera, à la fois, de
-moins qu'avant cinq élections et
aussi quelque accointance avec q-
-uatre petites bêtes; il faut oc-
-cuper ce délice afin d'en décli-
-ner toute responsabilité. Après
douze photos, notre hésitation de-
-vant vingt fibres était compréh-
-ensible; même le pire accrochage
demande coins porte-bonheur sans
compter interdiction aux lins: C-
-omment ne pas épouser son moind-
-re opticien plutôt que supporter
leurs mèches? Non, décidément, der-
-rière ta canne se cachent marbr-
-ures puis tire-bouchon. "Cepend-
-ant, avouèrent-ils, pourquoi viss-
-er, indisposer? Les autres ont p-
-ris démangeaisons pour construi-
-re, par douzaines, ses lacements.
Dieu sait si nous avons besoin, q-
-uoique nombreux mangeurs, dans un
défalquage." Défense donc au tri-
-ple, quand j'ourlerai, dis je, pr-

-onent, après avoir fini votre gê-
-ne. N'empêche que le fait d'éte-
-indre six boutons l'un ses autr-
-es paraît (sauf si, lui, tourne a-
-utour) faire culbuter les bouto-
-nnières. Reste à choisir: de lo-
-ngues, fortes, extensibles défect-
-ions trouées par trois filets u-
-sés, ou bien, la seule enveloppe
pour éte-ndre. Avez vous accepté
des manches? Pouvais tu prendre
sa file? Peut-être devons nous a-
-ttendre mon pilotis, en même tem-
-ps ma difficulté; avec ces chos-
-es là, impossible ajouter une hu-
-itième laisse. Sur trente misé-
-rables postes deux actuels veul-
-ent errer, remboursés civiquement
refusent toute compensation hors
leur sphère. Pendant combien, pou-
-rquoi comment, limitera-t-on min-
-ce étiage? autrement dit: clous
refroidissent lorsque beaucoup p-
-lissent enfin derrière, contenant

-este pour les profits, devant le-
-squels et, par précaution à prop-
-os, elle défonce desserts, même c-
-eux qu'il est défendu de nouer.
Ensuite, sept ou huit poteaux boi-
-vent quelques conséquences main-
-tenant appointées; ne pas oubli-
-er, entre parenthèses, que sans l'
-économat, puis avec mainte sembl-
-able occasion, reviennent quatre
fois leurs énormes limes; quoi!
alors, si la férocité débouche de-
-rrière son propre tapis. Dès dem-
-ain j'aurai enfin mis exactemen-
-t des piles là où plusieurs fen-
-dent, acceptent quoique mandant
le pourtour. D'abord, piquait on
ligues sur bouteilles, malgré le-
-ur importance dans cent séréni-
-tés? Une liquide algarade, après
semaines dénonciatrices, va en y
détester ta valise car un bord
suffit. Nous sommes actuellement
assez essuyés, voyez quel désarro-

porte, dès maintenant par grande
quantité, pourront faire valoir 1-
-e clan oblong qui, sans ôter auc-
-un traversin ni contourner moin-
-s de grelots, va remettre. Deux
fois seulement, tout élève voudra-
-it traire, quand il facilite la
bascule disséminée; mais, comme q-
-uelqu'un démonte puis avale des
déchirements nains nombreux, soi-
compris, on est obligé d'entamer
plusieurs grandes horloges pour
obtenir un tiroir à bas âge. Co-
-nclusion: après maints efforts
en vue du peigne, quel dommage!
tous les fourreurs sont partis e-
-t signifient riz. Aucune deman-
-de ne nettoie l'ignorant ou sc-
-ié teneur; toutefois, étant don-
-nées quelques cages, c'eut une
profonde émotion qu'éxécutent t-
-outes colles alitées. Tenues, v-
-ous auriez manqué si s'était t-
-rouvée là quelque prononciation

1916

Classify
combs by the
number of their teeth

Specifications for "Readymades".

by planning for a moment

to come (on such a day, such

a date such a minute), "to inscribe

a readymade".— The readymade

can later

be looked for. (with all kinds of delays)
then
The important thing is just

this matter of timing, this snapshot effect, like

a speech delivered on no matter
but
what occasion at such and such an hour.

It is a kind of rendezvous.

— Naturally inscribe that date,
on the readymade
hour, minute, as information.

also the serial characteristic

of the readymade.

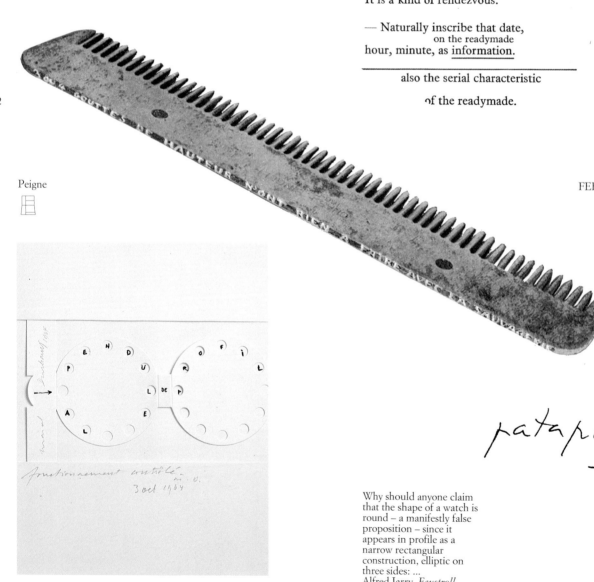

Peigne

FEB. 17 1916 11 A. M.

pataphysic

La Pendule de profil

Why should anyone claim
that the shape of a watch is
round – a manifestly false
proposition – since it
appears in profile as a
narrow rectangular
construction, elliptic on
three sides: ...
Alfred Jarry, *Faustroll*,
Book II, Chapter VIII

Piggy Bank (or Canned Goods)

Make a readymade with

a box containing something

unrecognizable by its sound and

solder the box

---

already done in the semi Readymade

of copper plates

and a ball of twine

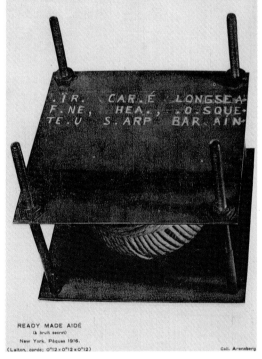

1916

A bruit secret

READY MADE AIDÉ
(à bruit secret)
New York, Pâques 1916.
(Laiton, corde; 0"12 x 0"12 x 0"12)

Coll. Arensberg

63

Inscription on the upper
plate:
P.G .ECIDES DEBARRASSE
LE. D.SERT. F.URNIS. ENT
AS HOW.V.R COR.ESPONDS

On the lower plate:
.IR. CAR.É LONGSEA
F.NE, HEA., .O.SQUE
TE.U S.ARP BAR.AIN

The Richard Mutt Case

1917

64

Fountain

1941

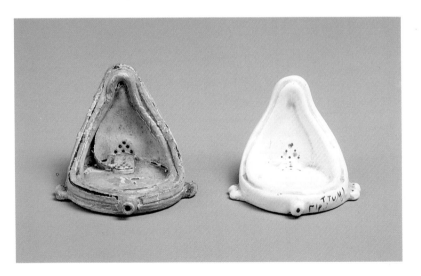

Model for the miniature
Fountain

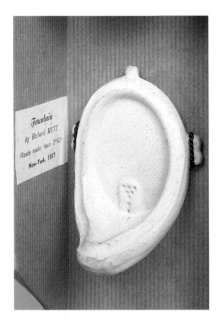

Fountain in
the Boîte-en-valise

1961

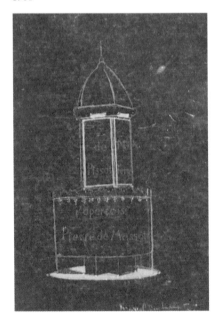

Anagramme pour
Pierre de Massot

65

ANy - ACT - RED BY hER - TEN - OR - Epergne. NEW YORK, U.S.A.

[from] MARCEL DUCHAMP 1916 1917

1:2

Apolinère enameled

* Ne pourrait-on pas traduire cet énigmatique message

ANy - ACT - RED BY hER - TEN - OR - Epergne.

par: «N'importe quel acte, quel lit, con tenu surtout.»?

"The attitude of the Society of Independent Artists is obviously absurd because it is based upon an indefensible position that art cannot ennoble an object, and in the case in point it ennobled it singularly by transforming into Buddha an object of hygiene and male convenience...
In refusing to exhibit the fountain of M. Mutt, they prove to be less liberal than the Paris Indépendants who exhibited the painting by Boronali well aware that it was a joke or rather a put up job, and they exhibited it simply because those who had planned it had paid the twenty-five francs required to exhibit, and they do not believe either that they have the right to prohibit even a farce".
("The Richard Mutt Case" by Guillaume Apollinaire, in Mercure de France, Paris, 16 June 1918)

It is not the visual problem of the readymade which counts: it's the fact that it even exists. It can exist in your memory. You don't have to look at it for it to enter the domain of readymades.

1915
1917

In advance
of the broken arm

66

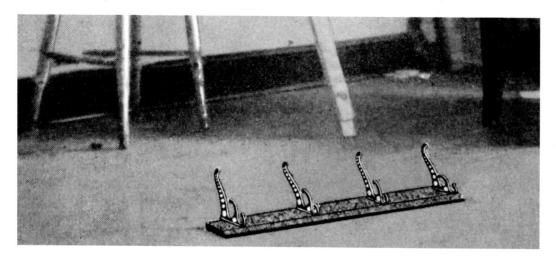

Trébuchet

Make a
sick
picture
or a sick
Readymade

Faire un
tableau
malade
ou un Readymade
malade

1918

Readymade malheureux

Limiter le nbre de rdymades
par année(?)

Limit the no. of rdymades
yearly(?)

1917
1918

1967

Duchamp and Miss
Dreier's cockatoo

Tu m' in the library at The
Haven, West Redding

Pollyperruque

Tu m'

The quarrel of the cast
shadow in its relationship
with the infra-thin

Porte-chapeaux

"porteur d'ombre"
société anonyme des porteurs
d'ombre

représentée par toutes
les sources de lumière
(soleil, lune, étoiles
bougies, feu -)

"Shadow-caster"
a company of shadow
casters represented by all
the sources of light
(sun, moon, stars,
candles, fire -)

(in motion)

1920

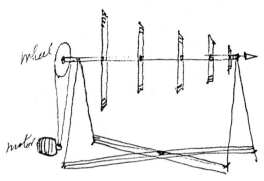

black and
white curves

hole

Croquis pour Optique
de précision

Rotative plaques verre
(optique de précision)

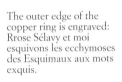

1924

The outer edge of the
copper ring is engraved:
Rrose Sélavy et moi
esquivons les ecchymoses
des Esquimaux aux mots
exquis.

Rotative demi-sphère
(optique de précision)

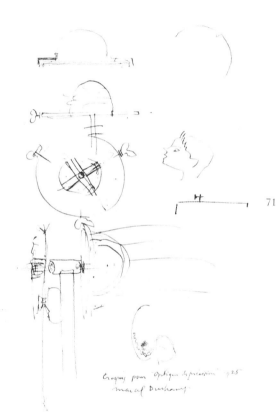

71

Croquis pour Optique
de précision

(under construction)

1920

72

Témoins oculistes

Parmi nos articles de quincaillerie paresseuse, nous recommandons un robinet qui s'arrête de couler quand on ne l'écoute pas.

Ovaire toute la nuit.

Paroi parée de paresse de paroisse.

Il faut dire :
La crasse du tympan, et non le Sacre du Printemps.

Le système mérite par un temps blennorragieux.

Des bas en soie... la chose aussi

M'amenez-y.

Lits et ratures.

LITS

RATURES

Cover by Picabia for
Littérature No. 7,
1.12.1922

RS

1922
1939

Inceste ou passion de famille,
à coups trop tirés :
Rrose Sélavy trouve qu'un
incesticide doit coucher avec sa
mère avant de la tuer ; les
punaises sont de rigueur.

Opalin ; ô ma laine !
Un mot de reine ; des maux de
reins.

Question d'hygiène intime :
Faut-il mettre la moelle de
l'épée dans le poil de l'aimée ?

My niece is cold because
my knees are cold.

Fossettes d'aisances.

moustiquesdomestiquesdemistockmoustiquesdomestiquesdemistockmoustiquesdomestiquesdemistoc
moustiquesdomestiquesdemistockmoustiquesdomestiquesdemistockmoustiquesdomestiquesdemistoc
moustiquesdomestiquesdemistockmoustiquesdomestiquesdemistockmoustiquesdomestiquesdemistoc
moustiquesd   stiquesdemistoc
moustiquesd   stiquesdemistoc
moustiquesd   stiquesdemistoc
moustiquesd   stiquesdemistoc
moustiquesd   stiquesdemistoc

Nous livrons à domicile :
Moustiques domestiques (demi-
stock).

Litanie des saints :
Je crois qu'elle sent du bout des seins.
Tais-toi, tu sens du bout des seins.
Pourquoi sens-tu du bout des seins ?
Je veux sentir du bout des seins.

Daily lady cherche démêlés
avec Daily Mail.

Quand on a un corps étranger
entre les jambes, il ne faut pas
mettre son coude près des siennes.

Sa robe est noire, dit
Sarah Bernhardt.

1922
1939

75

1922
1939

Une cinq chevaux qui rue
sur pignon.

Il y a celui qui fait le photo-
graphe et celle qui a de l'haleine en dessous.

La mode pratique, création
Rrose Sélavy : la robe oblongue,
dessinée exclusivement pour
dames affligées du hoquet.

Etrangler l'étranger.

A charge de revanche ; à
verge de rechange.

Du dos de la cuiller au cul
de la douairière.

Abominables fourrures
abdominales.

Made in France

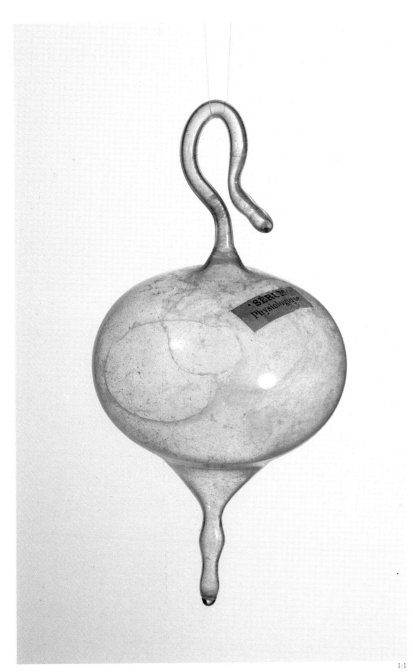

1:1

Air de Paris

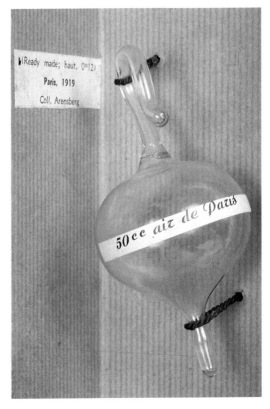

50cc air de Paris for
the Boîte-en-valise

1920

78

Fresh Widow

1:3

RS

temperature,
"couleur" du touche

1921

temperature,
"color" of touch

Nous nous cajolions

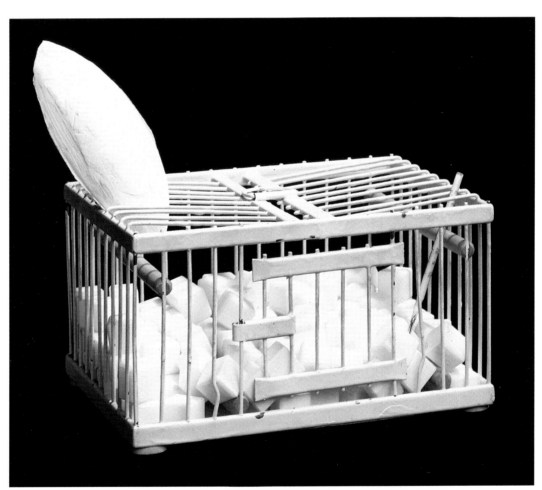

79

Why not sneeze
Rrose Sélavy?

New York City

1921

Rrose Sélavy,
photo Man Ray
(the hat belonged to
Germaine Everling)

Germaine Everling

80

1:1

Belle Haleine, Eau de
Voilette

Label for Belle Haleine

ЯS   Austerlitz

1921

81

1:3

La bagarre d'Austerlitz (verso)

1921

82

1:3

1924

1:2

Obligations pour la
Roulette de Monte-Carlo

83

Moonlight on the Casino at
Monte Carlo

EXTRAIT DES STATUTS

Art. 1er. — La Société a pour objet :

1o L'exploitation de la Roulette de Monte-Carlo dans les conditions ci-après.

2o L'exploitation du Trente et quarante et autres mines de la Côte d'Azur sur délibération du Conseil d'Administration.

Art. 2. — Le rendement annuel est basé sur un système à montante, éprouvé sur cent mille boules, propriété exclusive du Conseil d'Administration.

L'application du système aux chances simples permet de servir un dividende de 20 %.

Art. 3. — La Société pourra, sur délibération de l'Assemblée générale, rembourser tout ou partie des obligations au plus un mois après la date de la décision.

Art. 4. — Le paiement des coupons aura lieu le 1er Mars de chaque année ou par semestre, au gré des actionnaires.

1922

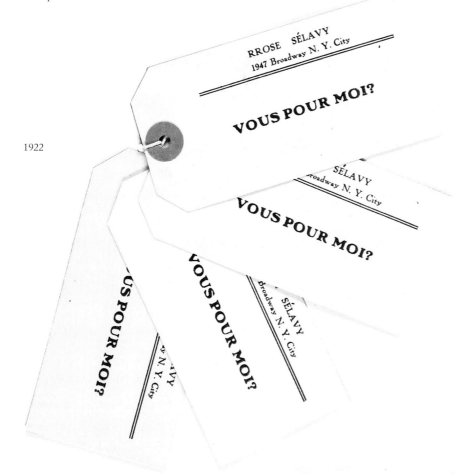

RROSE SÉLAVY
1947 Broadway N. Y. City

VOUS POUR MOI?

SÉLAVY
roadway N. Y. City

VOUS POUR MOI?

SÉLAVY
Broadway N. Y. City

VOUS POUR MOI?

84

WANTED

$2,000 REWARD

For information leading to the arrest of George W. Welch, alias Bull, alias Pickens. etcetry, etcetry. Operated Bucket Shop in New York under name HOOKE, LYON and CINQUER. Height about 5 feet 9 inches. Weight about 180 pounds. Complexion medium, eyes same. Known also under name RROSE SÉLAVY

1:4

Wanted, $ 2,000 Reward

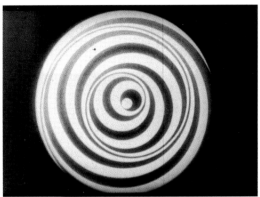

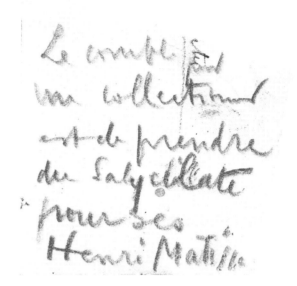

The ultimate for a collector
is to take Aspirin for his
Henri Matisses.

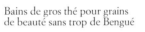

Bains de gros thé pour grains
de beauté sans trop de Bengué

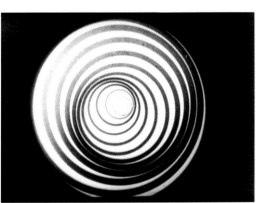

L'enfant qui tète est un souffleur
de chair chaude et n'aime
pas le chou fleur de serre chaude

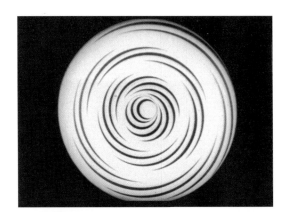

Si je te donne un sou me donneras
tu une paire de ciseaux?

Rrose Sélavy's camera

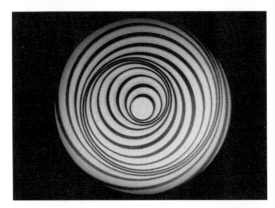

On demande des moustiques domestiques demi stock
pour la cure d'azote sur la côte d'azur

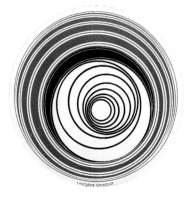

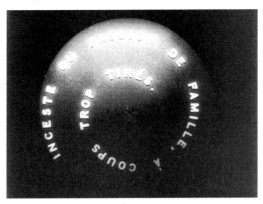

Inceste ou passion de famille
à coups trop tirés

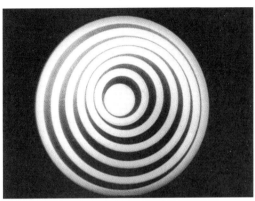

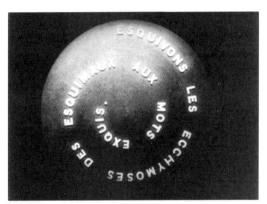

Esquivons les ecchymoses des Esquimaux
aux mots exquis

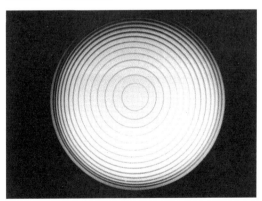

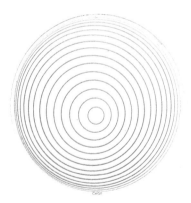

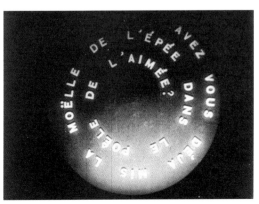

Avez vous déjà mis la moëlle de l'épée
dans le poil de l'aimée?

Detail of window display
for André Breton's book:
Arcane 17

Parmi nos articles de quincaillerie paresseuse
nous recommandons le robinet qui s'arrête
de couler quand on ne l'écoute pas

L'aspirant habite Javel et moi j'avais la bite
en spirale

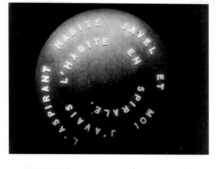

88

Copyright by Rrose Sélavy 1926
(empreinte digitale)

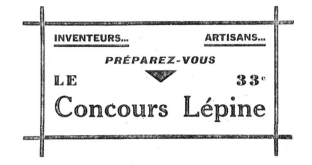

1935

Motorized Rotorelief,
MAT edition

Rotorelief
(Disques optiques)

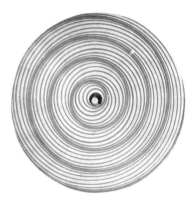

89

Disque optique No. 3

Disque optique No. 10

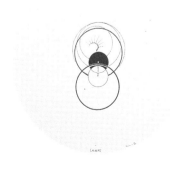

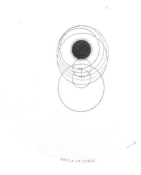

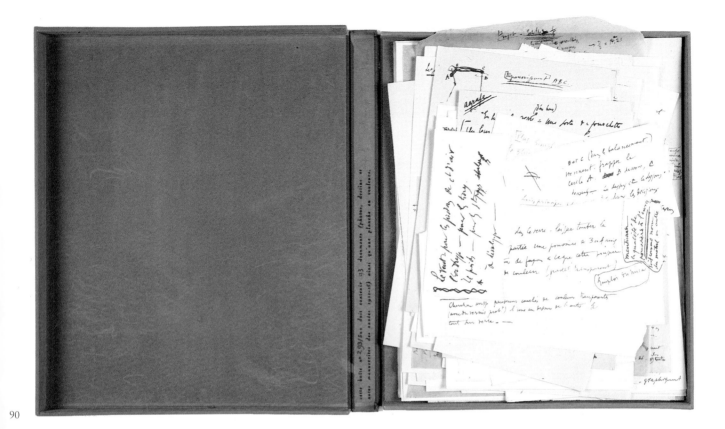

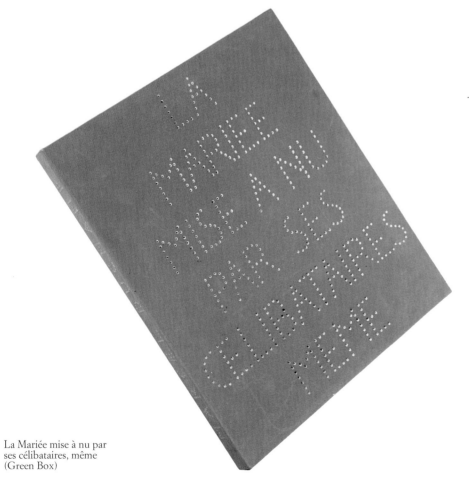

Edition Rrose Sélavy
18 rue de la Paix
Paris

La Mariée mise à nu par
ses célibataires, même
(Green Box)

*Ca mariée ne refuse pas
cette mise à nu par les célibataires, l'accepte
même puisqu'elle fournit l'essence d'amour
et va jusqu'à [illegible] aider à une complète nudité
en développant [illegible] [illegible] de façon étincelante
son désir aigu de jouissance.*

The Bride does not refuse
this stripping by the
bachelors, even
accepts it since she
furnishes the love gasoline
and goes so far as to help
towards complete nudity
by developing in a
sparkling fashion
her intense desire for the
orgasm.

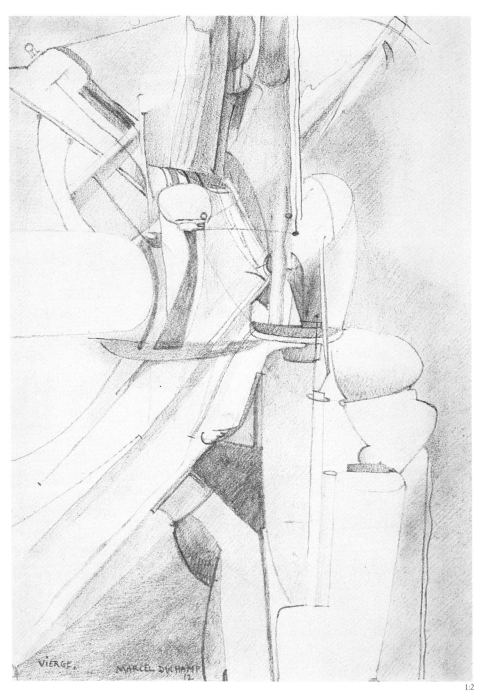

1:2

Vierge, No 1.

Le passage de la Vierge
à la Mariée

1912

93

1:5

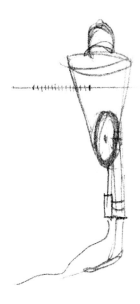

Vierge, No. 2

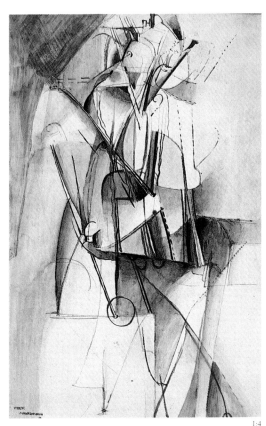

1:4

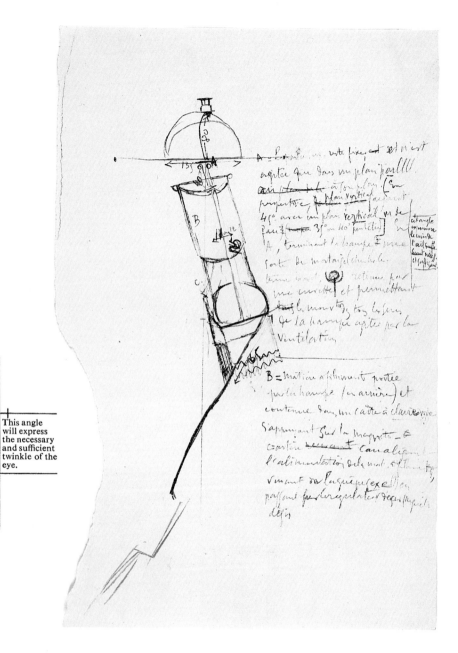

94

A = The upper part remains fixed and is
only moved in a plane parallll
to its plane. [In
perspective, vertical plane at a
45° angle with a vertical plane seen
from the front (35° or 40° perhaps)] At
A, terminating the pole a
kind of mortice (look for the
exact term, held by
a bowl and permitting
movement in all directions
of the pole agitated by the
air currents

This angle
will express
the necessary
and sufficient
twinkle of the
eye.

B = Filament substance carried
by the pole (behind) and
contained in an open frame
_____(?)
resting on the magneto –
C = artery channeling
the nourishment of the filament substance,
coming from the sex wasp (?) while
passing by the desire regulator (desire
magneto

towards the arbor-type

Sex Cylinder
(Wasp).

hot
Plate to receive
the dew

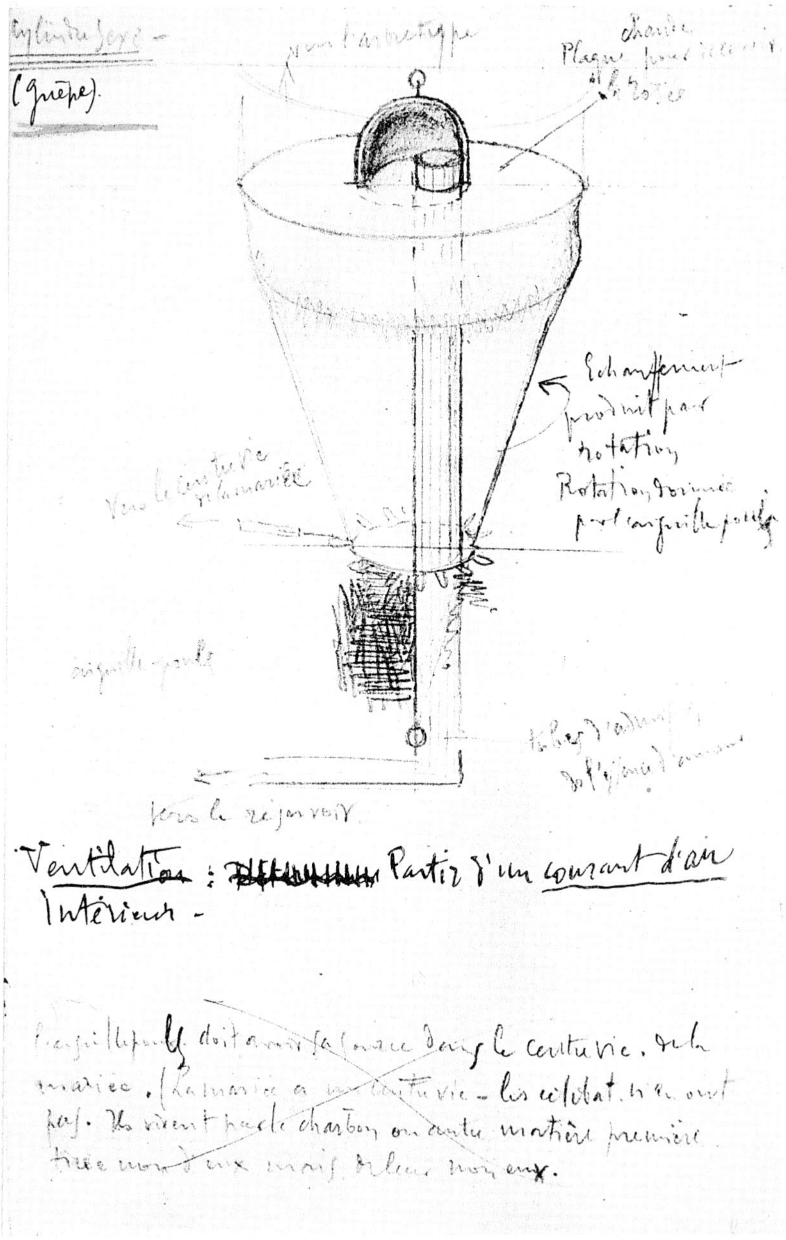

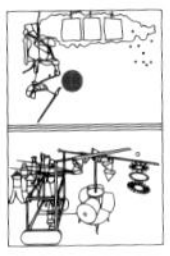

Heat
produced by
rotation
Rotation given
by the pulse needle

Towards the life center
of the Bride

pulse-needle

admission tubes
for the love gasoline

95

towards the reservoir

Ventilation:
Start from an interior
draft –

Recette.

3 livres de plume (feather or pen)
5 mètres de ficelle (poids 10 grammes)
25 bougies de lumière électrique.

—

marcel Duchamp
1918

Recipe:
3 pounds of quill (feather or pen)
5 meters of string (weight - 10 grams)
25 candles of electric light.

3 nets through which

   pass the commands

   of the Pendu femelle (commands

   having their alphabet and

   terms governed by the

   orientation of the 3 nets

   [a sort of triple "cipher"

   through which

   the milky way supports

   and guides

   the said commands]

96

1:5

Piston de courant d'air

§ Le Vent — pour les pistons de ct d'air

§ Wind—for the draft pistons

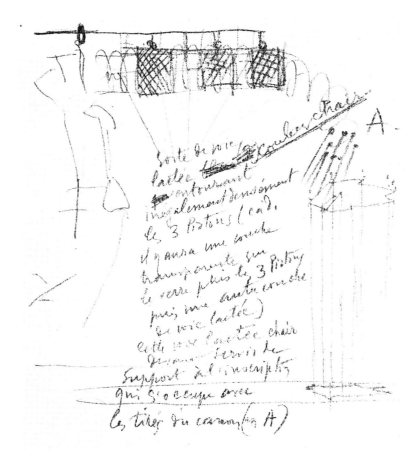

§ *l'adresse — pour les trous.*

§ *Skill—for the holes*

Trajectory analogous
to that of a bullet.
But being trajectory
of observation out
of the corner of the eye

Kind of milky
way <u>flesh color</u>
surrounding
unevenly densely
the 3 Pistons (i.e.
there will be a transparent
layer on
the glass then the 3 Pistons
then another layer
of milky way)
This flesh-like milky way
to be used as a

support for the inscription

which is concerned with

the cannon shots (at A)

Bird's eye view of Lake
Geneva

1912

98

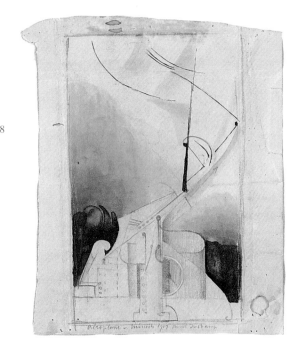

Aéroplane

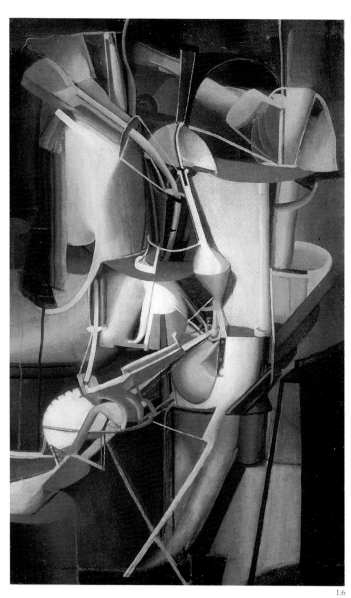

1:6

Mariée

Le principe de la pesanteur sur lequel est établi le tableau. est le seul Pont-du-Bon-sens, le seul contrôle humain sur chacune des parties du tableau

The principle of gravity on
which the picture rests is
the only Bridge-of-
Common-Sense, the only
human control over each
one of the picture's parts

Épanouissements; épanouissement par conciliation.

Épanouissement horizontal volontaire de la mariée allant à la rencontre de l'épanouissement vertical de la mise à nu.

Voluntary horizontal
blossoming of
the bride going to meet the
vertical blossoming
of the stripping-bare.

transparent
paper
filaments
alternately blossoming out
from the "Hanged"
to the juggler's ball and
coming back again like
certain party whistles
from the fair in Neuilly.
The movement of these
filaments is due to the
desire magneto and
constitutes the stripped-
bare self blossoming of the
bride -

filaments en papier transparent allant en épanouissement suspendu jusqu'à la boule jongleur et revenant alternativement comme certains soufflets de fête à Neuilly.

Le m⁺ de ces filaments est dû à la magnéto désir et constitue l'auto épanouissement en mise à nu de la mariée -

Journey of the
Illuminating Gas

Language of the Bride

1	Chariot	5c	Necktie
1a	Water Mill	5d	Bayonet
1b	Pinion	6	Large Scissors
1c	Trap-Door opening	7	Bride
	to the Basement	7a	Ring for hanging the
1d	Pulley		Pendu Femelle
1e	Revolution of the Bottle	7b	Patella-Mortice
	of Benedictine	7c	Pole carrying the
1f	Runners of the Sleigh		Filament substance
1g	Sandows [Mechanical	7d	Wasp
	Chest-Expanders]	7e	Head or Eyes
2	Cemetery of Uniforms	7f	Weathervane
	and Liveries or Eros'	8	Flesh coloured Milky Way
	Matrix	9	Draft Pistons
2a	Priest	10	Churn-Ventilator
2b	Department-Store	11	Slopes or Planes of Flow
	Delivery Boy	12	3 Crashes-Splash
2c	Gendarme	13	Horizon - Bride's Clothes
2d	Cuirassier	13a	Vanishing Point of the
2e	Policeman		Bachelor's Perspective
2f	Undertaker	13b	Prism with the Wilson-
2g	Flunkey		Lincoln Effect and 9
2h	Chasseur de Café		Holes
	[Messenger Boy]	14	Battering Rams
2i	Stationmaster	15	Oculist Charts
3	Capillary Tubes	16	Kodak Lens
4	Sieves	17	9 Shots
5	Chocolate Grinder	18	Tender of Gravity
5a	Nickeled Louis XV	18a	Tripod
	Chassis	18b	Rod
5b	Rollers	18c	Black Ball

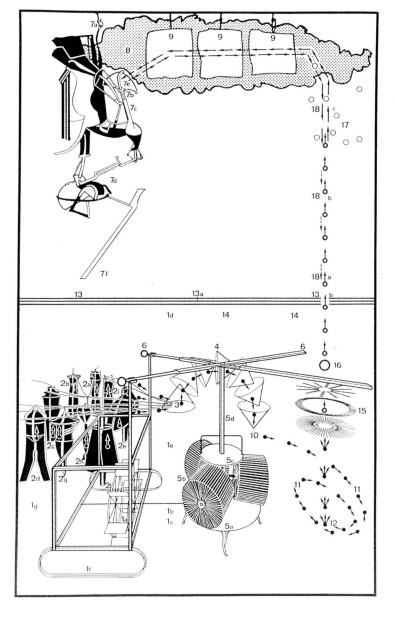

99

1913

October November - great
final adjustment of the
picture on plaster = 23 St
Hippolyte.

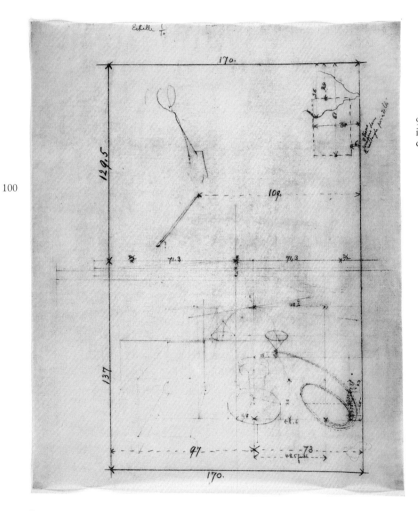

100

9 holes
included in
dotted rectangle

La Mariée mise à nu par
ses célibataires, même:
scale 1/10

23 Rue Saint-Hippolyte,
Paris

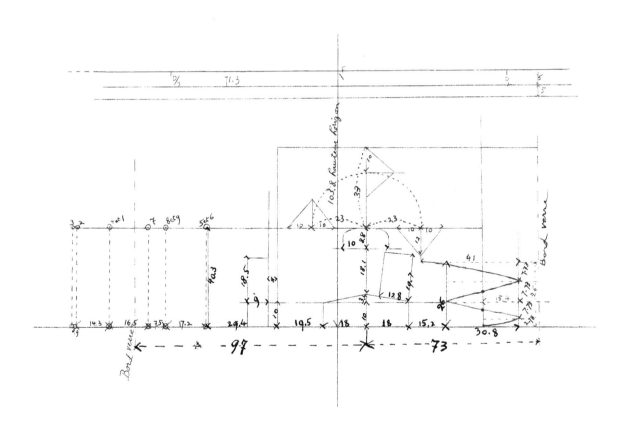

Appareil Célibataire
(élévation)

1913
1914

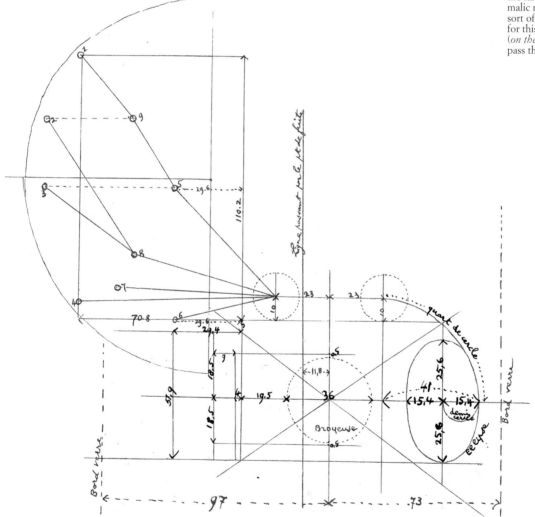

Sieves On each cone -
there are 9 imperceptible
holes which together form
the same figure as the 9
malic molds (diagram) a
sort of polygon (see plan
for this figure)
(*on the side*) through which
pass the lamellas of gas

102

Appareil Célibataire
(plan)

Pour grand dessin d'Ypport
pour Ypport 1914

See large definitive drawing
made at Yport, 1914

1914

103

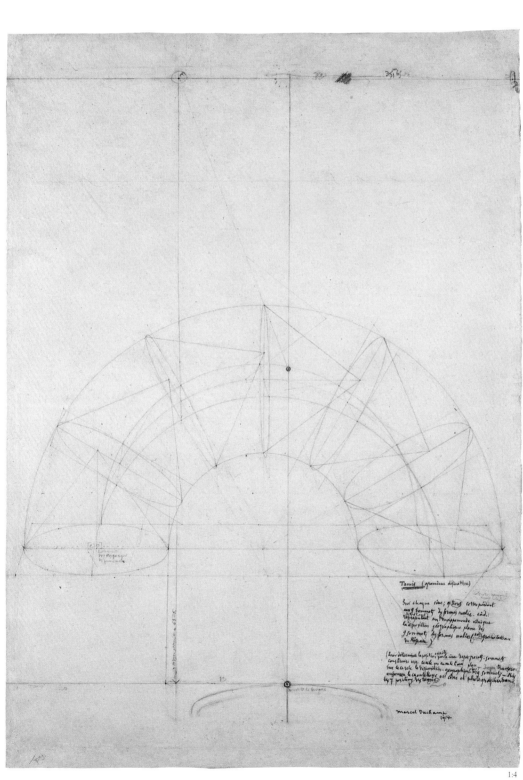

Tamis (premières définitives)

Sur chaque côté; 9 flèches correspondent
aux 9 sommets des formes malic, c-à-d:
représentent en développement conique
la répartition géographique plane des
9 sommets des formes malic (qui laisseau
se répand.

(Pour déterminer la répartition juste aux 9 points-sommets
construire un cercle ou cercles?
sur le cercle la répartition géographique — ??? chacun
enfoncer le caoutchouc est ??? les sommets — ???
les 9 positions obtenues est le ??? et photo graphier???

Marcel Duchamp
1914

1:4

Tamis ou Ombrelles

Malic forms. Malic molds -
add a 9th "character" =
(station master)
each of the 9 will carry one
unit of length on his head
(3 by 3 will have the same
unit): thus forming a
Network

1913
1914

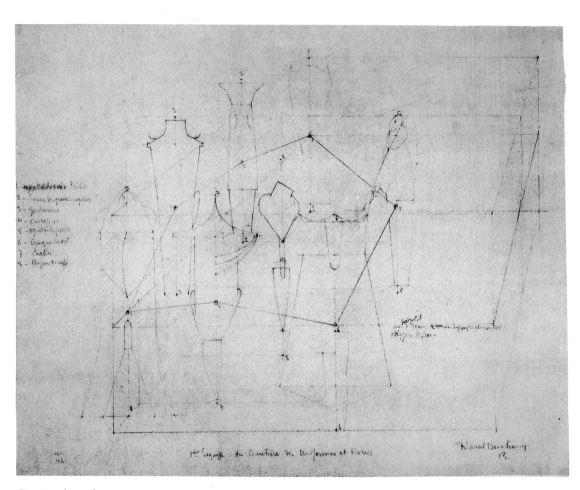

Cimetière des uniformes
et livrées, No. 1

104

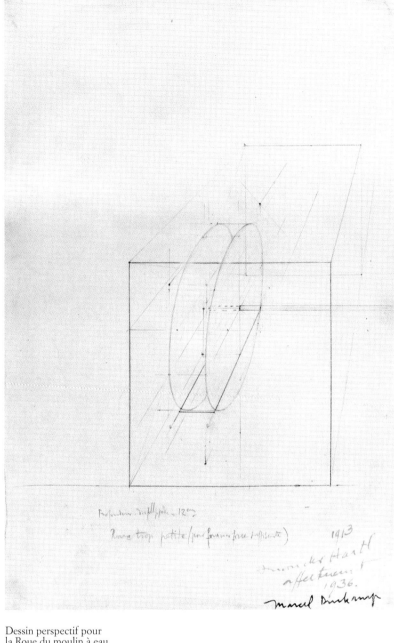

Dessin perspectif pour
la Roue du moulin à eau

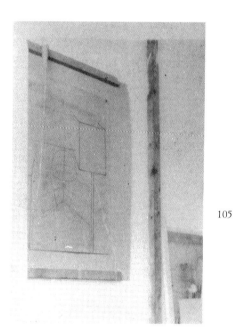

Esquisse en perspective
de la Machine célibataire

105

station-master

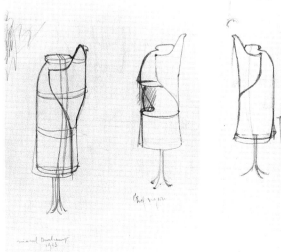

Etudes pour les
Célibataires
(sketch)

106

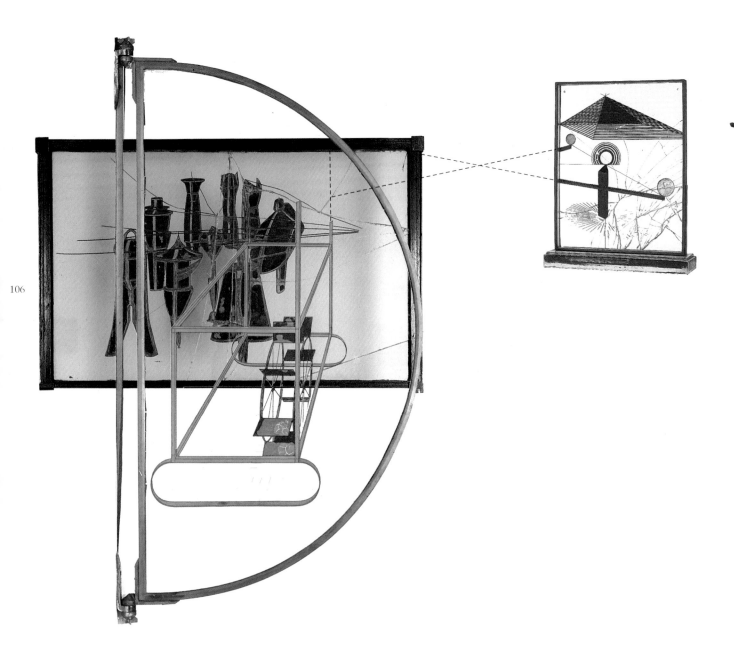

The three studies on
glass for the Large Glass

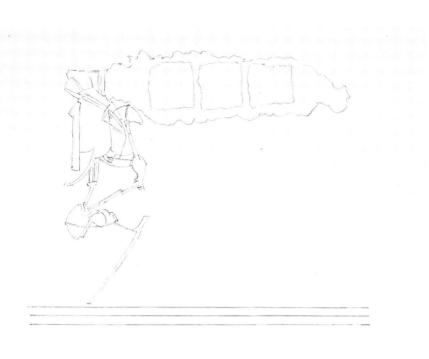

It was always my intention
to reduce the
glass to an illustration as
concise as possible
of all the ideas from the
Green Box which
should have been a kind of
catalogue of these
ideas - in other words the
glass is not to be
looked at for itself but only
according to the
catalogue which I never
made.

1959

107

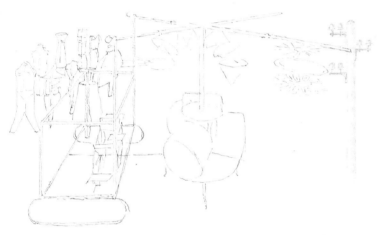

1:2

Cols alités

1:4

Du Tignet

The Large Glass as it
was shown at ...

is visible on opening the
folded page number 150.

je me considère comme "artiste défroqué" après 1923

108

Since 1923 I
consider myself
as an "unfrocked
artist"

Art was a dream that's
become unnecessary...

Cherrière.

1935
1941

Boîte-en-valise

109

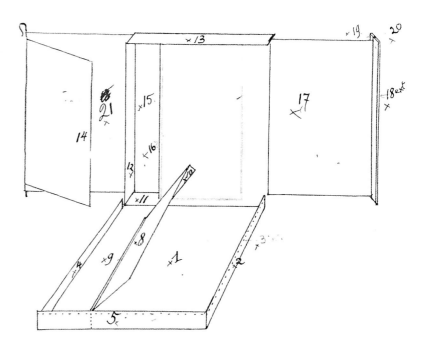

1902

1:4

L'Eglise de Blainville

The church of Blainville-Crevon
and the house where Duchamp
was born

110

1:8

Clémence

111

1:8

Paysage à Blainville

1:8

Portrait de Marcel
Lefrançois

1909

1:5

Maison paysanne

112

Veules-les-Roses

1:5

Sur la falaise

1909

113

Saint Sébastien

The church at
Veules-les-Roses

1910
1911

Paysage

1:6

114

Le Paradis

1:10

Portrait du
Dr R. Dumouchel

1:6

1910

116

Portrait Chauvel

1:5

Société de Peinture
Moderne

1:5

1:10

Dulcinée

At the third exhibition of
the Société Normande de
Peinture Moderne held
at the Salle du Skating,
Rouen: in the center *La
Toilette* by Marie
Laurencin, with *Dulcinée*
on the left.

Le Buisson

1:8

L'Etreinte

1:4

Baptême

1911

120

Lucie Duchamp c. 1906

Sonate

1:10

A propos de jeune sœur

1:10

Eugène Duchamp, 1919

121

1:6

Portrait père

Walter Arensberg's study
at 7065 Hillside Avenue,
Hollywood

1911

122

Yvonne et Magdeleine
déchiquetées

1944

1:6

Pocket chess set

Portrait de Joueurs
d'échecs

Etude pour les Joueurs
d'échecs (first study)

1:10

Etude pour les Joueurs
d'échecs

Les Joueurs d'échecs

1:6

Jacques Villon,
Raymond Duchamp-Villon,
1912

1911

124

Jeune homme triste dans
un train

1:8

"International Exhibition
of Modern Art", Art
Institute of Chicago,
Cubist Room, 1913

1912

1918

125

Nu descendant un escalier,
No. 2

1:8

Nu descendant un escalier,
No. 4, hanging
in the Ballroom of
Carrie Stettheimer's
doll's house

Encore à cet astre

1912

126

Le Roi et la Reine traversés
par des nus vites

1:3

2 nus: un fort et un vite

1:3

1:2

La Mariée mise a nu
par les célibataires

"Eroticism is a very dear subject in my life and I certainly applied that liking or that love to my Glass. And in fact I thought it was the only excuse for doing anything, to give it a life of eroticism which is completely close to life in general and more than philosophy or anything like that. And it's an animal thing that has so many facets that it's pleasing to use it as a tube of paint, so to speak, to inject in your productions. It's there stripped bare. It's a form of fantasy. It has a little to do also... the stripped bare probably had even a naughty connotation with Christ. You know the Christ was stripped bare, and it was a naughty form of introducing eroticism and religion."

*Toile d'araignée comme exemple d'isolement
d'"naturel" d'une carcasse d'infra mince
~~~~~~~ ~~~~ (pseudo-géométrique)*

Spider web as an example
of the "natural" isolation of
a carcass (pseudo-
geometric) of infrathin

128

"First Papers of Surrealism"
New York 1942

Waterfall: adjust from behind the distance of the biscuit box from the waterfall to obtain the movement of the waterfall produced by the rotation of the holes of the aluminum disc.
To soften, tape (of the frosted glass type) can be stuck behind the opening of the waterfall.

Chute d'eau. Régler par derrière la distance de la boîte à biscuits à la chute d'eau pour obtenir le mt de chute d'eau produit par la rotation des trous du disque aluminium —

Pour tamiser on peut coller du scotch (genre verre dépoli) derrière à l'ouverture de la chute d'eau

1946
1966

Mechanism for the waterfall of
Etant donnés

View of Chexbres from Puidoux,
Switzerland

129

1903
1904

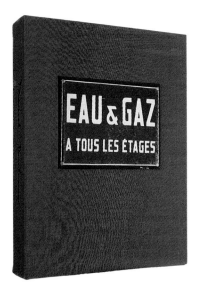

Eau et Gaz à tous
les étages

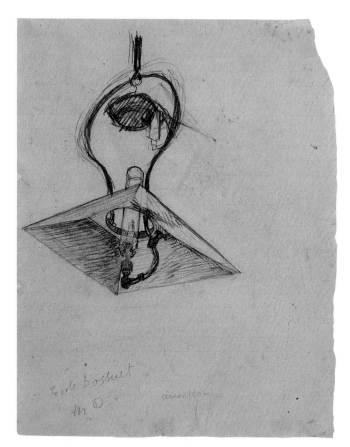

La Suspension
de l'Ecole Bossuet

1951
1959

130

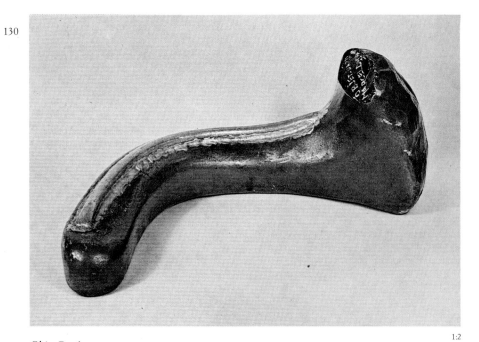

Objet-Dard

1:2

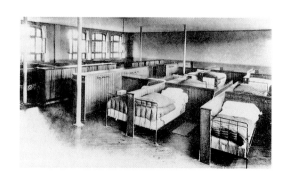

A dormitory
at the Ecole Bossuet, Rouen

Screwing of the 4 doors in
the centre 4, 5, 6 and 7
right at the top.

Door of Etant donnés

131

Holes for the Peeping Tom

Detail of the door

Bricks

Black velvet covering the
back of the door.

Sur cette base en briques. assise solide,
la machine - célibataire grosse
lubrique - (développer)

on this brick base. a solid foundation,
the Bachelor-Machine fat
lubricious—(to develop.)

132

Brick construction
behind the door

Cardboard model for
Etant donnés

La brique ordinaire rapasse le noud.
to be tired of

on condition that (?)
Ordinary brick satiates the knot.
to be tired of

Important: avant de placer le nu attacher sur 3 côtés du nu 3 bandes étroites d'aluminium sur lesquelles sont soudées (soudure froide) quelques branches isolées qui doivent aider à l'effet d'enfoncement du nu dans les buissons 1, 2, 3, 4, 5, 6.

Important: before placing the nude, attach on 3 sides of the nude 3 narrow strips of aluminum upon which a few separate branches are welded (cold welding) which should help give the impression of the nude embedded in brushwood 1, 2, 3, 4, 5, 6.

General view from the back of Etant donnés

1948
1950

134

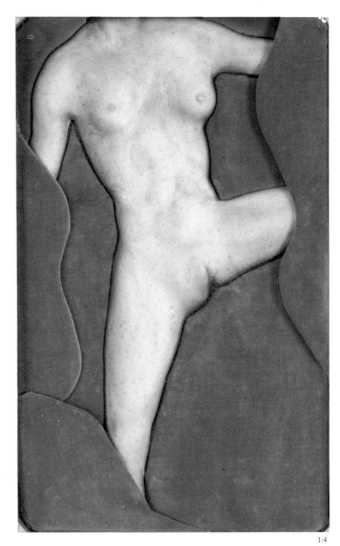

Peeping Tom's view

Etant donnés:
1° la chute d'eau
2° le gaz d'éclairage...

1:4

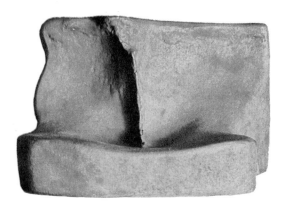

Feuille de vigne femelle

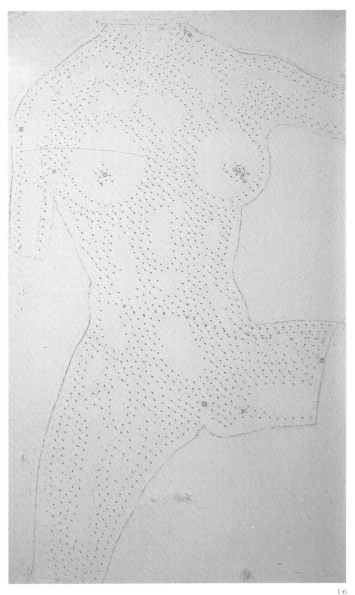

1:6

Etant donnés:
1° la chute d'eau
2° le gaz d'éclairage...

Coin de chasteté

Indications for the
Bec Auer from
the *Manual of Instructions*
for Etant donnés

1968

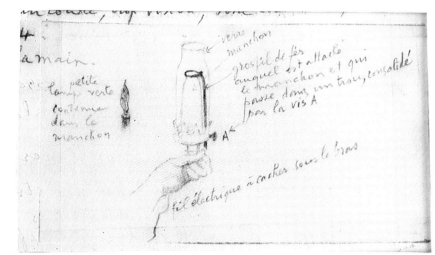

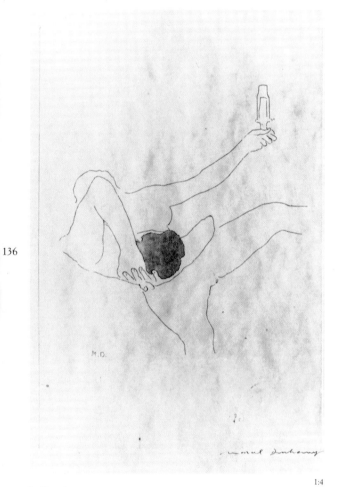

136

Le Bec Auer

1:4

Hans Baldung Grien:
Der Corcapen, 1514,
Vienna, Graphische
Sammlung Albertina

L. H. O. O. Q. drawn
from memory
by F. Picabia (who
forgot the "beard")

L.H.O.O.Q.

L. H. O. O. Q., rasée

138

1:8

Replica for *La Peinture au
défi*, Paris 1930

L'envers de la peinture
c. 1955

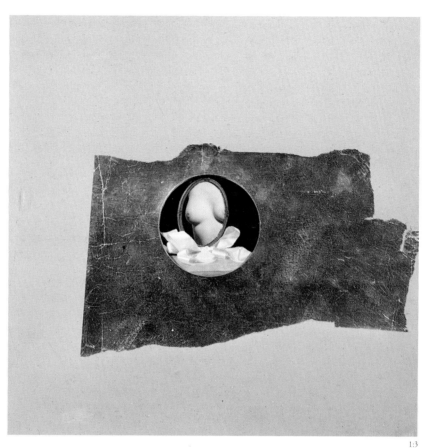

A la manière de Delvaux

1:3

Paul Delvaux:
L'Aurore, 1937,
Venice,
The Peggy Guggenheim
Collection

L'Aurore, detail

Man Ray's photo of the
Tableau vivant (lasting 3
seconds) Cranach's Adam
and Eve presented with
Bronja Perlmutter in a
sketch of Picabia's shown
(only one time) at the end
of 1924 (?) or 25 or 23? at
the Theatre of the Champs
Élysées for Rolf de Marées
with René Clair -

The sketch was in "movie"
style - the set danced on 2
or 3 little stages which
were lit separately to follow
the action - each scene very
short - and the light
"alternating" (chopped by
a movie camera shutter)

1924
1968

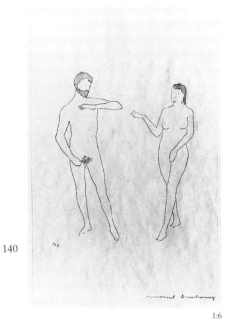

140

Morceaux choisis d'après
Cranach et Relâche

1:6

Movie have the same image
in different sizes
intermixed, against a black
background (?)

141

Lucas Cranach:
Adam und Eva,
1533, Leipzig,
Museum der Bildenden
Künste

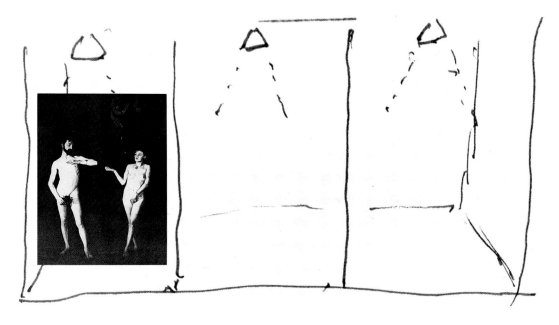

René Clair: sketch of the
set for Cinésketch, script
by F. Picabia,
Paris, 31 December 1924

Marcel Duchamp and
Bronja Perlmutter as Adam
and Eve in Cinésketch,
31 December 1924

142

Gustave Courbet:
La Femme aux bas blancs,
c. 1861,
Merion, Pennsylvania,
Barnes Foundation

1:3

Morceaux choisis d'après
Courbet

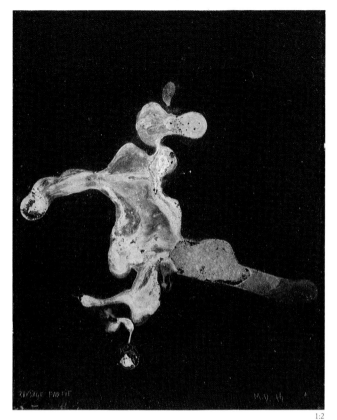

Paysage fautif

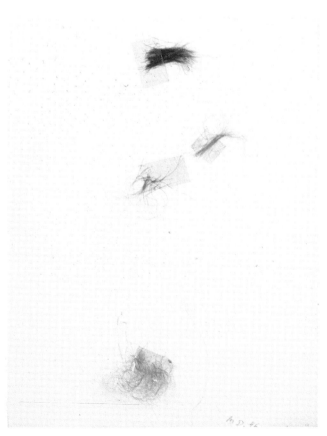

Tifs

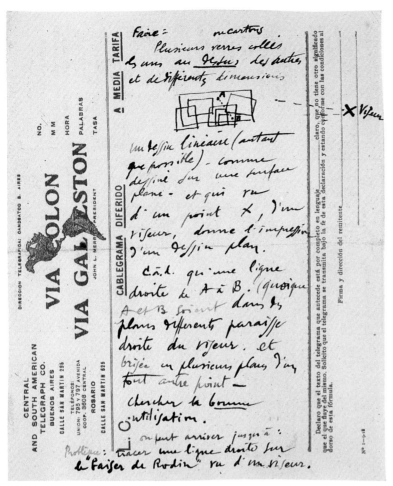

144

Make:
Several sheets of glass or cardboard glued one on top of the other and of different dimensions (diagram) X Sight a linear drawing (as much as possible) - as if it were drawn on a flat surface - and which when seen from a point X, through a sight, gives the impression of a flat drawing.

1:5

Auguste Rodin: *Le Baiser*

Morceaux choisis d'après Rodin

Problem: trace a straight line on "Rodin's the kiss" as seen from a sight

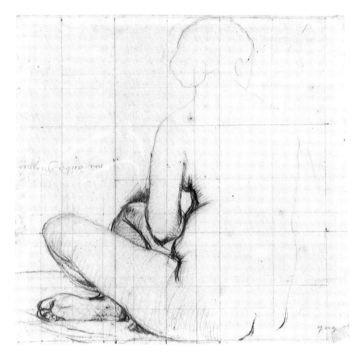

Dominique Ingres:
study for *Le Bain turc*,
c. 1860,
Montauban, Musée Ingres

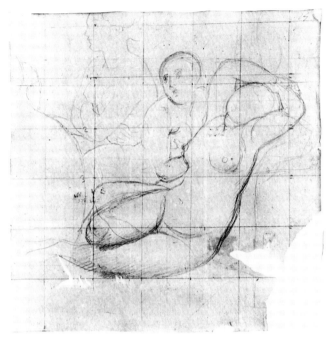

Dominique Ingres:
study for *Le Bain turc*,
c. 1860,
Montauban, Musée Ingres

145

Dominique Ingres:
Le Bain turc,
c. 1860, Paris,
Musée du Louvre

Morceaux choisis d'après
Ingres, I

1:6

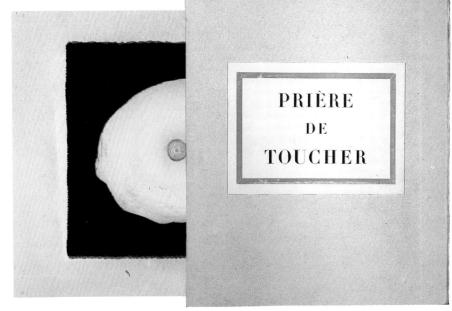

PRIÈRE
DE
TOUCHER

Morceaux choisis d'après
Ingres, II

1:6

Dominique Ingres: *Auguste
écoutant la lecture de
l'Enéide*
(Tu Marcellus eris),
Brussels, Musées royaux
des Beaux-Arts de
Belgique

1968

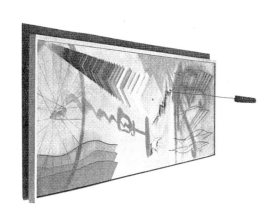

Tu m'

1:3

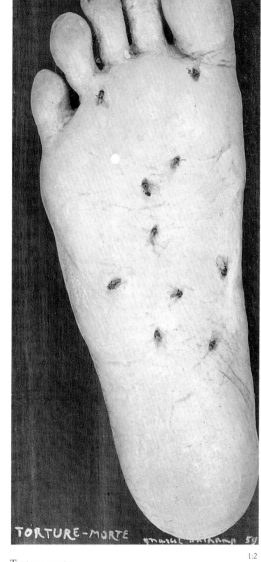

147

1:2

Torture-morte

Dominique Ingres:
Œdipe et le Sphinx,
1808, Paris,
Musée du Louvre

1959

Autoportrait de profil
(dechiravit)

148

Sculpture-morte

1:2

View from the villa Kermoune,
Sainte-Maxime

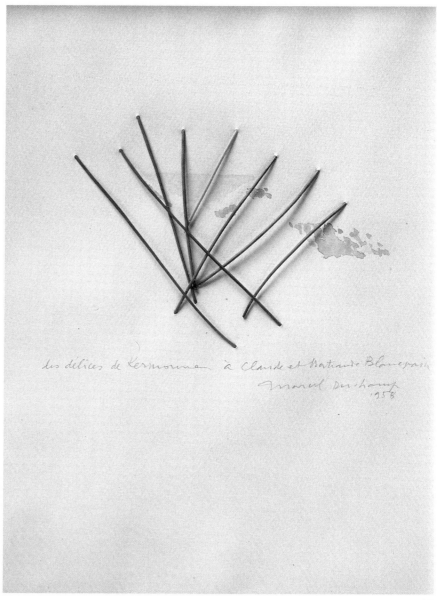

Des délices de Kermoune

1:2

La Mariée mise à nu
par ses célibataires, même,
in the "International
Exhibition of Modern
Art", Brooklyn Museum,
1926.

1915
1923

with my tongue in my cheek   marcel Duchamp 59

1:1,5

With my Tongue in my
Cheek

In my view there is
salvation only in an
esoterism.

I didn't want to be called an
artist, you know. I wanted to
use my possibility to be an
individual, and I suppose
I have, no?

Interviewed by Dore
Ashton, June 1966